13.25

BEFORE THE
AFRICAN STORM

by John Cookson

THE BOBBS-MERRILL COMPANY · INC.

Publishers

Indianapolis · New York

FIRST EDITION

ACKNOWLEDGEMENTS

IN THE compilation of the passages in this book which deal with current political developments in British Africa, I owe an immense debt of gratitude to Hugh Latimer, Colin Legum, John Worrall, J. Halcro Ferguson, Harry Franklin and other expert observers and interpreters of the African scene. The dispatches sent by these gentlemen to the London *Observer* and the controversies their observations have stimulated have been invaluable in the formation of such judgments as I have made.

I am indebted to the *African World* of London for most of the statistics quoted, while historical notes on Stanleyville and the Katanga are based on my translations of the writings of André Scohy, René Cornet, and the ruggedest individualist I have ever had the pleasure of knowing, Henri Ancelot.

JOHN COOKSON

RECOMMENDED READING

The works of Alan Paton and Stuart Cloete

Cecil Rhodes—a study by Emil Ludwig

The Expansion of Europe—Ramsay Muir

Congo—André Cauvin and Jean Latouche (Excellent pictorial study)

Struggle for Africa—Vernon Bartlett

CONTENTS

THE STORM CENTER

BEFORE THE AFRICAN STORM

Prologue: Makoko

ONE HOT, lazy morning in 1950, as I sat Chez Armand in Leopoldville sipping an iced anisette, Jean-Marie came in with a purposeful look. It was not yet ten o'clock but the humidity was already at saturation point. I was tired; I had been working all night on Radio Leopoldville with my coeditors Tillière, Verhulst, Ribeiro and Federico Guarddon, selling Belgium and the Belgian Congo to the Americas in French, Nederlands, Spanish, Portuguese and English. With the Belgian national anthem, *La Brabançonne*, still pulsating in my head, I wanted no part of Jean-Marie, but he bore down on me, his shoulders hunched, his huge head thrust forward.

Jean-Marie was a gangling Frenchman from Brazzaville. Without any affectation whatever he wore the heaviest black shell-rimmed glasses I ever remember seeing. He always wore sandals and the shortest of shorts, and once every ninety days he permitted himself the luxury of a pudding-basin haircut. Jean-Marie was a

13

parisien through and through—shrewd, brilliant, coldly logical and completely irresponsible. He was a twentieth-century Zola, a special pleader and, like all his race, a vigorous parlor and wine-shop politician, easily capable of thinking up and justifying a splinter party whenever he felt the slightest need to deviate from the position he happened to be holding at any given time. By the same token he spent many an evening with fellow *libres-penseurs* tilting at the Pope and his Cardinals, or playing "Bishop Puff," a mildly blasphemous round-the-table drinking game; yet I once saw him take a cognac bottle to the head of a serious Protestant who politely questioned the validity of the doctrine of the Immaculate Conception.

I was resigning myself to an exposition of the iniquities of the latest French government as he sat down, took a sip from my glass, rolled the liquor reflectively round his tongue, then called for an anisette for himself. But Jean-Marie's mind was relatively uncomplicated that day.

"Do you want to come with me to see a native funeral?" he said.

"I've just seen one," I replied. I had in fact just passed a forlorn little party on its way to the cemetery. I saw again for a moment the men moving ahead at a fast walk with the coffin, the women, some of them with babies slung on their backs, trying to keep up with the pallbearers in a hop, skip and jump fashion while shrilly goading their older offspring who loitered even farther to the rear.

But Jean-Marie cut into my reflections: "*Nom de*

Dieu," he said. "This is a royal funeral. Didn't you see my column in the *Equateur* last night? The Makoko is being buried *là bas* tomorrow."

Jean-Marie nodded toward the French side of the Congo River. And that is how, two hours later, I found myself sitting in the back of an old French Army truck which had been pulled up with typical African unconcern about three inches from the steaming banana-scented quayside at Brazzaville. With six others, including Jean-Marie, I sat hemmed in by iceboxes, photographic apparatus, recording machines, spare wheels and shovels, squirming under a throbbing lemon-yellow sun veiled in a copper sky.

As we began our long climb into the highlands behind Brazzaville, those monstrous black clouds—clouds seen only in the tropics—were piling up on the eastern horizon. It was late September and the weather was beginning to break. The sun was returning from its trip across the equator to take summer to northern lands; the dry, dusty equatorial winter was ready to give way to tropical downpours, and while we were still within sight of Brazzaville, the deluge came. The first real rain of the season accompanied us as we sped along, and it was not until many hours later as we leveled off on the plateau a few miles to the south of our destination that the torrent began to ease. When our sodden truck squelched through the quagmire into the native city, the thunder was rolling off to the southwest toward the river, and the sheets of lightning were getting pinker and so weak that they failed to silhouette the edges of the thunderclouds piled up on the sky line. And so we came to 'Mbé, where the Makoko of the Bateke had come home to die.

The Bateke are one of the more thriving and wide-spread peoples of Central Africa, and though their capital city 'Mbé is a cluster of reed-thatched mud-and-wattle huts on an arid tableland in French Equatorial Africa, I have met members of this tribe as far afield as the Belgian Katanga, 1,200 miles to the southeast. As we dismounted, Jean-Marie, now our self-appointed guide—he was, after all, the only Frenchman in our party—was laboring heavily with a disjointed account of how the Bateke were first identified about 1880 by the French explorer Count Savorgnan de Brazza, who declared their territory a French protectorate and made a treaty with the Makoko on the bank of the Congo where Brazzaville now stands.

"Makoko," which is a hereditary title signifying "king," set out to meet the French government mission, coming, as Jean-Marie put it, "in peace." There was no reason, declared Makoko—and Jean-Marie—why the white man and the black man should be enemies, and since that day the Bateke have lived in peace, an industrious and intelligent people, held in respect by the lesser peoples around them. This final claim I can substantiate, for my cook-boy Simon, a detribalized Kikongo from Boma on the Belgian side, once said of a friend: "He's a fine man," adding by way of sufficient explanation, "He's a Bateke." And it is equally true that the real enemies of these fine people have not been the white man and the knife and spear of tribal warfare, but the mosquito and the tsetse fly. Malaria and sleeping sickness have taken a heavy toll down the centuries; but now, with new drugs and some knowledge of hygiene, and watched over by the officers of the Institut Pasteur—one of Brazzaville's few reminders of the twentieth century—the Bateke are once more on the increase.

As we entered the village the good folk of 'Mbé were just emerging from their huts; night fires were being lighted, canisters of black tobacco and pitchers of banana beer were appearing from the shadows behind the door-ways. In the gathering night the Bateke squatted around their hearths. As yet shy and not a little resentful at the intrusion, they gave us no official welcome, but as we walked among them offering cigarettes and candy timid smiles began to appear. Then, somewhere in the dark-ness, someone began a dirge. Just two or three phrases, endlessly repeated, growing more and more insistent. The whole village was singing now, and the unsteady murmuring lilt became something massive as the emotions of the villagers took a firmer grip. There was savagery in the air, a tenseness poised behind the din.

'Mbé is little more than a wide place in the road. Orig-inally a crossing of jungle trails, the city is well placed strategically, and that is what these people had first to consider when choosing sites for their settlements. 'Mbé dominates the terrain in all directions; it lies high—and dry—above valleys of tall, rank grass, which can cut deep into clutching fingers, and flat-topped shade trees which lean away from the prevailing wind. The only serious drawback is the water supply. One of the village elders told me that a water party has to be organized every morning to fetch buckets of mountain water from a creek which runs through a valley about two miles to the north of the town. When the womenfolk go down to do the community wash, a bodyguard of men, armed with antiquated sporting guns, spears, knives, scythes and sticks, goes along to keep away the wild beasts which prey on the mountain antelope as they come down to water.

Just off to the west of the crossroads the main street of 'Mbé opens into a square, and in the center of this area—which serves as a weekly market place—stood the catafalque of Makoko. But at this stage the people of 'Mbé were paying it little attention. Their dirge continued to swell; they seemed self-absorbed and in no mood to answer a lot of questions, so I went over to the truck, got out my bedding roll and prepared to make myself comfortable until the morning. But I had reckoned without the music, and the music of the Bateke makes up in volume what it lacks in melody. They have no stringed instruments, nor do they use even the simplest wood winds: their chants, repetitious at all times, have an eerie monotony which is heightened by a battery of tom-toms of different sizes and pitches. So I got up again and went over to the musicians. They were just tuning up, and in much the same way as violinists take a few preliminary plucks at their strings these folk try out their tom-toms for pitch. The vellum of their primitive drums, usually antelope or gazelle hide, is stretched tightly over a wooden cylinder and held on by nonadjustable waxed cords.

Variations in tone caused by excess damp or undue stretching or contraction are adjusted by applying blobs of tar to the drum face. These tar balls are whittled down or added to, depending on just which tone the drummer wants, and for ten minutes or so there was the usual native hubbub while things were being fixed; then silence as the battery prepared to go into action.

The steady throb began. It was a signal to sing and dance: the young and nimble began gradually to jump and shuffle themselves into a frenzy; the old and stiff sat around listening, humming and puffing contentedly at little metal pipes containing harsh, uncured, black tobacco. The climax of the evening was approaching. It was now about midnight and the moon was high. The noise of the drums died down, the singing ceased, and just as I was thinking this must be all, four young men in grass skirts appeared and began to shuffle around one of the larger fires. One of them suddenly broke from the ring and did a rapid, hard-stamping run across the burning logs. A second crossed in the opposite direction, then a third and a fourth. They wove an intricate pattern to and fro, half kicking, half stamping at the blaze. In about three minutes the fire was completely out. Then the singing and the drumming began all over again. I was drowsy; I began to feel slumber coming on me and made once more for my bed. Not so the Bateke, who went to work with renewed vigor and whose voices, hoarse but willing, were the first sounds I heard when I emerged at half past six in the morning from a tom-tom-drugged sleep.

The morning was fine, and the altitude and the freshness made it quite chilly, a welcome change from the
torturing heat and damp of the riverbank. As I walked
into the square the dancing was still in progress, but it
was a tired imitation of the enthusiastic shuffling and
leaping of the night before. I moved across to the
djonchele, the catafalque, where quite a crowd was already gathering. It was a structure about nine feet high
with a base like a cutoff pyramid and a cylindrical top.
The base part was merely a pedestal; the body, in a sitting
position, was in the cloth-wrapped cylinder, which, when
it was dismounted later, looked something like an oversized cotton bale. A framed death certificate hung from
the catafalque:

> Makoko Kima Ilo, Paramount Chief and King
> of the Bateke. Returned to his Royal Abode on
> February 13th: died on April 28th, which was
> on a Wednesday, at six in the evening. Burial
> September 13th. Given under the hand of his
> nephew 'Nguie.

Meanwhile a more than usually disheveled Jean-Marie
had appeared. "See," he said, squinting at the notice,
"Makoko died in April, yet here it is September and he
hasn't been buried yet. *Mais ce n'cest rien*, it's nothing,
he's been 'smoke-cured.'" Then, reverting to his academic manner: "These Bateke know nothing of embalm-
ing, and in normal circumstances they bury their dead
within twelve hours after passing away. On this occasion
there was a great difference: headmen of the tribe had

to be summoned to the funeral from as far away as Katanga. There had to be tribal conferences and these, in Africa, can last for months. So, for such great occasions as this, the Bateke have adopted the simplest preserving process known. Smoking!"

At this point we fell in with a French-speaking Bateke, a dry-goods-store clerk from Brazzaville, who told us what he knew and spared us the guidebook phrases. It seems that immediately after death the corpse of Makoko was placed in a sitting position. It was clothed in its finest raiment and bedecked with bracelets and jewelry. The remains were then wrapped in cloth and finally tightly bound with lianas. The "bundle" was placed on a metal rack under which a fire of green logs was kept perpetually burning. Day after day the process of smoking went on until the body and all its organs became completely dehydrated and capable of preservation for an indefinite time. When this process was finished, new wrappings were added, the whole was built up into a cylinder, then mounted on the flat-topped pyramid, where it had stood, rain or shine, for many weeks before the burial.

The catafalque had fetish rags flying from the top to keep away evil spirits, while propped against the base were the king's spear and Onkou the war bell, a crude sort of cowbell which is sounded only as a declaration of war and which was last rung when De Gaulle's Free French declared war on the Axis. Along with Onkou lay Onaa, a conch shell which was reputed to give Makoko the power of hearing everything which was going on, even in faraway Brazzaville. A string encircled the cylindrical part of the "coffin," and from it were dangling a buffalo switch, the symbol of temporal power, a mirror (the only one in 'Mbé in all probability) and several photographs of which the most striking was an old daguerreotype of Savorgnan de Brazza. There were also a picture of Kima Ilo posing stiffly with the governor of French Equatorial Africa and, for no reason that I was able to determine, an ordinary snapshot of a Portuguese store in Brazzaville, with the fat proprietor standing in the doorway.

Meanwhile the crowd was growing; the tom-toms had resumed their pounding and the ritual dancers were beginning to sway. Some French newsreel photographers had managed to get their equipment into the square, and with an eye to business and a knowledge of the water situation, a family of Senegalese Moslems had set up a beer tent on the outskirts of the village.

The African has a keen eye for drama, and the suspense was being cleverly built up. Amid the mounting clamor and the posturings of the dancers, the village policeman could be seen getting to work hacking out a path through the sweating black skins. Suddenly, from the other side of the crossroads, a cry went up. It moved through the crowd toward us, and in a few seconds we were in the midst of a throng of natives shouting: "Galfuru! Galfuru!" The dowager queen of the Bateke had arrived.

The queen was a little old woman about four feet nine inches high. She wore a bright-crimson one-piece robe, a diagonal sash of very heavy scarlet silk, and carried a small ax as a sign of office. Pinned to her breast were two medals, one of which, I found out later, had been presented to Kima Ilo by General de Gaulle in recognition of his wartime loyalty. Galfuru walked up to the catafalque with a simple dignity unmarred by the fact that she was wearing a *topee* that had seen better days, sandals and bobby socks. Her face, deeply lined but not tattooed, was calm and set as, flanked by Bateke notables, she moved forward to the center of the scene.

Galfuru—"she who washes and makes clean the fire"—took from her pocket a small horn whistle, which she blew three times. Then she made a few passes in front of the catafalque to establish sympathy with the spirit of the late ruler, genuflected and remained for a few moments in silence. She slowly rose and walked back to her throne, a carved, collapsible wooden chair covered with a whole leopard skin. Bateke notables and members of the royal family were grouped around the throne, and before she sat down Galfuru made a short invocation while the group stood with bowed heads. Ivy-clad dancers appeared, the tom-toms came to life again, and a dance which I was told symbolized a victory for Makoko over his enemies began to a rapid, involved beat.

Then something happened which nearly reduced the day's ceremonies to burlesque. One of the courtiers produced a bottle of Pernod, a potent French liquor of the absinthe type, and Galfuru grasped the bottle, tilted it to her mouth and without so much as a blink began to swallow the stuff neat. We didn't know quite what to do, but we all seemed to decide that the best bet was to keep quiet—which we did. The bottle was put away and did not appear again. We found out afterward that it really *did* contain Pernod. And Galfuru claimed to be eighty years old!

The dancers continued to dance, the drums to throb, the cameras to whir, and an interpreter, more zealous than adequate, tried to help us interview the old lady. We did not have too much success; the interpreter with his rapid jabbering and bad French only succeeded in flustering her, and in addition Galfuru's memory was rather cobwebbed. We discounted her story of remembering De Brazza, but we did find out that she, as principal tribal matriarch, was the interim ruler and that, according to the law of many matriarchal tribes, of which the Bateke is one, the Makoko's successor would be chosen by ballot from the female side of the family— that is to say, the next Makoko would be the son of one of Kima Ilo's sisters or nieces. Galfuru then tried to give us the names of the tribal kings since De Brazza's time. She could remember five, but was contradicted by one of the notables. This started an argument, under cover of which we took our leave and retired to put our notes in some sort of order.

It was now eleven o'clock. The drummers had grown tired, and the leaf-clad dancers, no longer the center of attraction, had wandered off disconsolately into the crowd. Then a noise of orders violently given drew my attention back to the catafalque, where the bearers were taking their places. While the dancing had been going on, four long poles had been worked under the base of the structure. They protruded about eight feet at either end, making it possible for twenty-four bearers to take up position, three ranks of four in front with a duplicate arrangement behind. Here the lack of organization became still more obvious. The bearers had not been nominated previously and the usual haggle began, this time around the village gendarme, who struck a commanding figure in his neat white, gold-braided uniform and black French *képi* with a scarlet-and-gold top. His tactics were vague, though; it seemed as if he were shooing away the few who wanted to help and roping in those who stood indecisively around. It took some time and a great deal of breath to get the matter settled, but finally calm was restored and the unwieldy mass of the catafalque was raised on the shoulders of the bearers during one of the brief moments of silence that day.

They were a ragged lot, dressed for the most part in fragments of castoff European clothing. Some of them, no doubt as a sop to convention, wore grass skirts over their trousers. One wore an old British Army forage cap, another affected horn spectacle frames without lenses. There was little sorrow about the occasion and the procession tottered off amid songs and good-natured advice to the pallbearers. After the first twenty yards or so had been covered, the cortege came to a violent halt, backed a few paces, then went on again. At the village crossroads there was a similar occurrence. Each of the paths out of the village was tried until, coming back to the crossroads, the catafalque gave an even more dangerous lurch and had to be put down while the seriously enfeebled bearers wiped off the perspiration. Then a native girl, whose eyes were streaming with tears—the only display of real sadness I saw that day—walked up to the coffin, whispered a few words and caressed it gently.

I sought my Brazzaville dry-goods salesman again. He told me the catafalque behaved as it did because the spirit of Kimo Ilo did not wish the body to be buried. The crying girl was one of Makoko's younger wives, he said, and her soft words had soothed the spirit, which was now resigned to letting the corpse be dealt with according to custom.

So the procession, headed by the puffing and exhausted bearers, came to a hut on the edge of the village which had been specially prepared to receive the body. This little building had formerly been the dwelling of one of Kima Ilo's senior wives; that day it had been cleaned up, the walls had been decorated with ivy and banana fronds, and a deep circular grave had been dug in the center of the earth floor. Outside, the catafalque was shorn of its trappings. The pictures and ornaments were put to one side and the top was lifted from the base. Long liana ropes were placed under the part containing the corpse, and the coffin was moved slowly toward the doorway. Then, and only then, it was found that the door was too small, and the bearers had to leave their burden and set to work with machetes to make the entrance bigger. In the process they all but demolished the little house, but at least it became possible to get the clumsy bulk to the edge of the grave. The bearers, still exhorted by the leather-lunged policeman and still disposed to tell one

another the way everything should be done, at last succeeded in slowly lowering the coffin into the ground.

The lachrymose young wife reappeared. This time
the tears were theatrical: she wanted to recapture her
brief moment of glory, and with the searing yell of a
professional mourner she attempted to throw herself into
the grave. She was unceremoniously dragged off by an
older woman, presumably one of Makoko's elder wives—
or, rather, widows—and was given a very sound beating
while we stood around looking very sheepish, uncertain
how to handle a women's brawl. Jean-Marie, for a moment the chevalier, stepped in and separated them. The
shrieking youngster was led away by four very capable-
looking motherly women; her antagonist wandered off
alone and was quickly lost in the throng.

I looked around for Queen Galfuru, but she was not in
the hut. A moment later I saw her outside, talking to
the traveling priest who had arrived in the village that
day to say Mass for his handful of converts. That was the
last I saw of her. She took no part in the rather rowdy
committal proceedings: she stood aloof, a pathetic little
soul, looking for all the world like the Red Queen in
Through the Looking-Glass.

Earth was now being heaped on the coffin. The in-
signia and finery lay in a sad heap against the outside wall.
The ceremony was over, the dancers were stilled; a
lethargy had descended on the village. Kimo Ilo, Makoko of the Bateke, had been gathered to his fathers.

Jean-Marie was standing at my side, and as our eyes
met I could sense that he was thinking my thoughts with

me. We had been nearer to the soul of Africa that
morning than we had ever been before, or ever would be
again. Our experience had left us disappointed and not
a little apprehensive. Wherever the historic lingers on
in the Dark Continent, the twentieth century is at its
elbow piloting it toward the grave. Unless the journey
can be vested with a fitting dignity, the end may be violent and bloody.

Jean-Marie sighed. "Yet the change has got to come.
The new Africa demands it. Primitive economics—look
at the way they worship their cattle up in Ruanda. Primitive social structure. You know, sometimes I think it
might be better to get it over quickly, even if a few heads
do get cracked."

"But what exactly will you put in its place?" I asked.

"Eh! I honestly don't know yet, *mon cher.*"

My dear chameleon was a nihilist that bright Sunday
morning. I put an arm around his shoulders and steered
him back to the truck.

1

The Problem

I FIRST saw Africa in 1940. The world was again at war: France, Belgium, the Netherlands, Norway and Denmark had succumbed to the highly trained German war machine. Benito Mussolini was still ranting about what he would do to the British in the Near East, and Allied convoys were beginning to roll from the bleak northern waters across the equator, round the Cape of Good Hope, to Durban, and on up through the Mozambique Channel to Mombasa, Aden and Suez.

As a passenger on one of these gigantic sea caravans, I first became acquainted with Africa. Our ship, the old *Empress of Asia*, a monstrosity in maritime baroque which was shortly afterward to go down in the Indian Ocean, had lost touch with the convoy, and we arose in the morning to see a lone destroyer circling around us like an angry wasp. At breakfast it was announced over the intercom that the coast of Sierra Leone lay just below the sky line, and three hours later, our wonder mixed

29

with relief, we saw the purple-and-green mass of Sierra Leone—the Mountain of the Lion—raising its truly lion-like head above the waves. Gradually the shimmering white lighthouse and the palms, papaws and mangroves of the shore line detached themselves from the haze, while, as we rounded the boom, Freetown—a neat little city of screened-porch bungalows rising in orderly ranks up the hillside—filled in the blurred details of the first African canvas I had seen.

We stayed four days at Freetown taking on coal. The dust and the din soon dulled the edge of the rapture, but the sight of the African coast line with its vivid, unnaturally bright colors emerging as we crossed the harbor bar on a sweltering, cloudless noontide is as clear today as it was thirteen years ago.

When I finally took off from Cairo for London in 1946 I went with a heavy heart. Inside me was the knowledge that I had not seen enough of Africa and had barely begun to know it. I knew North Africa from Sinai to Algiers; I had seen a great deal of South Africa and had learned much more, while in the Near East, from British and Dutch South Africans and husky Zulus and Basutos of the noncombatant Pioneer Corps. I had loitered on the quayside at Mombasa and spent sleepless, insect-ridden nights in the Southern Sudan and Uganda. Yet I felt I knew so little, and there I was—former historian to the Middle East Command—bound for a Whitehall desk with nothing more exciting in view than a career as a war historian.

Since I knew the ground and could trace the Wadi Akarit and the Mareth Line blindfolded, I was assigned to a task which involved an autopsy of the Tunisian campaign, but the rigidly academic lines on which the story had to be conceived and written withered any vicarious pleasure I might have derived from writing again of the palm trees of Sfax, Gabès and Tunis and the blue Mediterranean. So my thoughts moved once more toward living in Africa, and I found myself within a year packing my trunks and heading south—this time to the Belgian Congo.

Based on Leopoldville, I spent the five happiest years of my life so far. The Belgian National Broadcasting Service, which is state-sponsored in much the same way as the British Broadcasting Corporation, was, and is, high on the list of those organizations which broadcast to the world in a babel of tongues. Hushed for a moment when the Nazis moved into Brussels in 1941, the voice of Belgium soon raised itself over powerful short-wave transmitters from Leopoldville, the capital of the Belgian Congo. After the war, programs on Belgian and African life, history, art and all forms of cultural expression—along with international news bulletins—continued to pour from OTC, *La Voix de la Concorde*, the Voice of International Good Will.

Thus, one muggy Saturday afternoon in the fall of 1947, I found myself, the new English editor for this cultural experiment, fastening my safety belt as the plane banked in a final semicircle over the steel-gray sheet of the Congo River to land on the Leopoldville runway. Five years later the appropriation I dreaded was voted by the Belgian government, new 100-kilowatt transmitters were installed at Wavre—the site of a lively skirmish just prior to the Battle of Waterloo—and our entire international family packed its typewriters, dictaphones and files and moved en masse to Brussels. Now the voice of OTC is stilled and a more metropolitan and sophisticated ORU has taken its place, but it is still *La Voix de la Concorde*, and speaks nightly to the world.

Much of the research I did for a series of African Colonial talks is finding more detailed expression in this book. The Belgian colonial authorities, to whom we had to submit our texts before publication or broadcasting, never blue-penciled any honest criticisms we made. And thrown together as we were—Belgian, French, Dutch, Spanish, Portuguese, Swedish and British, each and every one of us removed from his natural habitat— we spent months, nay years, studying colonial Africa in all its moods. It is small wonder that from time to time each one of us assumed the mantle of Nostradamus. I wonder how right, or how wrong, the future will prove us to have been.

In the fall of 1952 I said a fond farewell to Africa with the promise that I would soon be back, as I undoubtedly will. There is an old saying: "Those who drink the Nile waters always return." I have drunk the waters of the White Nile and the Blue Nile, the Congo, and Niger and the Zambezi; for me there is no escape. My feet have trodden dusty roads in all Africa's countries but Ethiopia and Somaliland; I have pitched my tent in Durban and

Leopoldville, Khartoum and Cairo, Tunis and Kano.

But the Old Africa Hand gives a special meaning to the word "Africa." Egypt is dismissed as a projection of the Levant, and the Sudan and Ethiopia go overboard with it. Libya, Tunis, Algeria, Morocco and to a certain extent the countries of Africa's western bulge do not qualify as truly African: the influence of Islam pervades them, and Arab culture—an Asiatic culture—is their dominant note. No, says your African veteran, Africa begins at 6° N and extends southward to the Cape. And, being somewhat of an Old Africa Hand myself, I hasten to agree, for the cultural, social and linguistic patterns of what, for want of a better general term, I shall call the Bantu lands are completely different from those of the Arab, Berber and Arabized Negro countries to the north.

The Bantu lands are what might be called the southern peninsula of Africa. They range from the fertile vine-yard-covered slopes of the southern Cape to the steaming jungles of the Belgian Congo and Uganda; from the lofty, deified heights of Ruwenzori to the damp, desert coast line of Southwest Africa, which lies shrouded in fogs brought on chill antarctic currents. And spread throughout these five million square miles are fifty million dark-skinned people speaking nearly three hundred related languages and dialects, knowing little of one another, yet sharing a common heritage of exploitation and oppression.

Whence came these Bantu? The word "Bantu" means simply "the people." Actually we know little about them.

The best that can be said is that they are "Negroid"—a term which specifies physical characteristics but which, so the pundits tell us nowadays, cannot be applied "racially." Liberally strewn with the primitive stock are admixtures of Nilotic, Arab and Hottentot blood, while to a lesser degree Chinese, Malay and Hindu strains have been assimilated. White Aryan peccadilloes are responsible for hordes of underprivileged mulattoes, rejected as neither fish, flesh nor fowl. The parent stock of the Bantu peoples is thought to have originated in Central Africa—though some claim their cradle is as far north as Nubia—and successive migrations have brought them by stages to the equatorial belt.

Yet whence the Bantu came is incidental. Where he is going is what really matters, for Central Africa, the paradise of romanticists, idealists, ethnographers, and men of business, might well become a decisive battleground in the ideological war between the free world and Communism. Less than a hundred years ago the center of Africa was a void on the map; eighty years ago the chart began to fill in with river and lakeside settlements; towns grew from pinheads to big black dots. Then came roads, railroads and finally air lanes, spun out like spiders' webs linking more and more cities, mines, factories and storehouses.

For eighty years ago an industrial revolution began in South Africa. Slowly, inexorably, it spread northward. The Rhodesias and the Belgian Congo long ago cast off their purely agrarian character and their rulers are now struggling to achieve a balanced industrial and agricultural economy. The European beckoned; the native followed him into the mines and factories. The new life created an African proletariat. Now a more poised, reflective African sees the European still for what he first was—an exploiter. The white man beckons again. This time he is the benevolent father. But is the African going to follow him into the maze of the social welfare programs he is preaching? Or is the African going to say: "Once a white man, always a white man," and point to men like Daniel Malan in the Union of South Africa and the federationists in the Rhodesias and London?

The colonial powers—the British, French, Belgians and Portuguese—who have divided Central Africa among themselves can see this writing on the wall: their spokesmen come to the African with open hands and sleeves turned back, faces shining with honesty. "Follow us," they say. "Work along with us and learn how to run your own countries. We will put you on the road to your inheritance. Let's face it. There will be dangers and difficult times ahead, but if you trust us we'll all win out."

I am sure there is no doubt that the colonial powers are speaking and acting in good faith, but I cannot help feeling that, with the situation developing in the way it is, they are staking too much on the political and social maturity of the African they have created. Another serious obstacle to the best-laid scheme may well be the large number of white pioneers, who, despite the ominous trend of events, have not allowed their consciences to give them any trouble. The traders, the miners and the engineers are proud of their new Africa as it pirouettes in blues, reds, whites and greens in the brilliant sunshine. Many of them want to cling to things as they are, for the sunny days bring forth energy; the buildings mushroom, the roads ribbon out, the mines spew forth uranium ores, gold, diamonds, copper, cobalt, manganese and tin. The forests yield their rubber and timber, the paddies their rice and the hillsides their coffee, tea and tobacco. Yet, there are still all too many Old Africa Hands with the exploiter mentality. Their fixed regard for the African as an on-the-spot, cheap source of labor has produced a blind spot for the counterinfluence of the emancipators. And these sons of the pioneers may yet awake one day to find energy dying in the stilling air, and the African frustrations of half a century welling up and swamping their work in a few hours of storm.

This is precisely what the Communists are waiting for. I've seen the Communist at work, his glib phrases falling on eager ears in the intervals between ping-pong games in native welfare clubs. His aim—world domination—in his eyes justifies any means. He is not hampered by scruples about acting in good faith. He has little to lose, for as yet he has accomplished little in Africa, and he can make his approach fit any set of circumstances. His Black Utopia, filled with Cabins in the Sky, he depicts in hard, even outlines. His is the short view, vying with that of the liberal reformer, who presents the grayer long view and who must in his honesty burden the unready African with a knowledge of the pitfalls along the road.

The future of Africa may be bright, but at present it is fraught with every possible danger. Everywhere there is an atmosphere of tension: blows and counterblows have already been struck in the mines and on the coffee plantations. It could well be that the whole world will become involved in the struggle to determine the spiritual and material future of the Dark Continent.

"The sins of the fathers shall be visited upon the children unto the third and fourth generation. . . ." This trite pearl, dropped one day by Jean-Marie, who like Beelzebub could quote Scripture for his own ends, drew from me the retort that the colonial powers are more to be pitied than censured for the present state of affairs. They are struggling to reverse the unpleasant legacy of a grossly materialist nineteenth century.

The colonial powers' decision to take up the struggle may be due to a belated attack of conscience, but there is not the slightest doubt in my mind that their actions are also conditioned by an awareness of what is good for them. Economic pressures on homeland and colony, political pressure at home and very wide differences in national temperament have led to the evolution of four quite different conceptions of the responsibilities of empire.

And here is the crux of the problem. Though the basic dilemma facing the colonial powers is the same one—the peaceful resolution of Africa's present difficulties—their approaches to it are very dissimilar. And it will be hard to reconcile these differences when the attempt is made, as it will have to be, to formulate an over-all policy for the future.

An attempt will have to be made to formulate an over-all policy? Yes, because otherwise the enemy will adopt specific tactics in each colony, and these territories will be lucky to escape falling, like ripe plums, piecemeal into his basket.

But the idea of outside influence being brought to bear is odious to all but the broadest liberals, and Britain and the others find themselves continually striving to placate influential foreign opinion while at the same time maintaining their privileged position in these African territories. Their colonies are, after all, the principal sources of what material prosperity two world wars have left them.

The measures of "appeasement" taken since the end of the First World War have at least been steps in the right direction. But African colonialism, it seems to me, is only a lid on a cauldron of boiling pitch. Sooner or later, as the black tide rises, this lid must be lifted gently to one side—or be blown off. The African intellectual, who because he can think and act both ahead of and along with his people, is their preferred leader and is beginning to see himself in a leader's role. It would be a rash man who would dare to predict that what happened in Indonesia only a few short years ago could not possibly happen in this continent of gigantic rivers, mountains, jungles and swamps. And there are all too many of us who, like Jean-Marie in his bewildered mood, sigh and say, "What is to come? I honestly do not know, *mon cher*."

This mixture of apathy and bewilderment is understandable, since the comparative luxury which characterizes the life of the European in Africa diverts attention from all unrest short of armed insurrection. The house-wife's day is rarely disturbed by anything more serious than the breaking of a dish, the boiling over of the coffee pot, or the need to intervene in a kitchen squabble. African politics, only sketchily understood in Europe and America, are played down also by the local press. International affairs, so it seems to me, are highlighted by African newspapers so that by inference Africa becomes a haven of peace and tranquillity. And it is so easy and pleasant for one sitting on the veranda of the clubhouse to chat idly of the mango rains, the outcome of the tennis tournament, or the I.Q. of the *moké* who tried to clean white suede shoes with black polish. Only very rarely do the merchants and planters rise to the bait of a political discussion: they leave such matters to their employees. The chatter of the country-club set in the new African cities consists of the same vapid nonsense as it does in America, for these people have the full bellies which create lazy minds.

But, thank God, there are on the other hand devoted government servants, educators, priests and ministers, who mix with the African, discuss his problems and do not let events get ahead of them. And though the ideals of these friends of the African may be similar, it is tragic that in the absence of a co-ordinated effort to tackle the dangers ahead they seem to be pulling away from each other.

The British, for example, follow what the journalists call the "middle of the road" policy. This phrase is sup-posed to mean that the Colonial Office in London, heed-

less of the clamor of the extremists among the Africans
and the British settlers, has embarked on a course which
will lead eventually to complete African self-determination. Each "evolved and responsible" Central African
country, with a freely elected multiracial legislature, will
have the choice between remaining within the framework
of the British Commonwealth or seeking its fortune as an
independent state. The means adopted to bring about
this end are not sensational. The evolution of the African
is to proceed in gentle stages, his political education keeping pace with his cultural and technical development.

Africans are already being given a greater voice in
town and provincial government, particularly in Uganda,
and their representatives have seats in the legislatures of
the British colonies and protectorates. This is an encouraging sign and the British, the most conscientious of administrators, have already shown good faith by granting
to the Gold Coast what is almost complete self-government under an African legislature—only the British
governor-general remains—while Nigeria is almost ripe
for similar treatment. The Anglo-Egyptian Sudan has
been granted the right to decide within the coming two
years whether its people want independence or integration with Egypt.

Burma established a precedent a few years ago when
its leaders elected to withdraw from the British orbit, a
move which has resulted in improved relations between
British and Burmese. It is far too early to say whether
the African colonies and protectorates will do the same
as Burma has done when they are finally asked, as they
surely will be, to make a similar choice.

The British territories in East Africa, which come within the scope of this book, are inhabited by the least advanced of Britain's subject peoples. European colonization came later on the east than on the west coast of Africa. There was no Suez Canal until 1869 and to reach what are now Kenya and Tanganyika the first European traders and explorers had either to sail around the Cape of Good Hope or attempt the treacherous Nile Valley route. The towns of the coast were in the hands of Arab adventurers or Arabized Negroes who were suspicious of white efforts to penetrate into the interior. Many of these Moslems sent slaves to the Near Eastern markets and quite naturally resented the presence in their midst of white men with humanitarian impulses. Many others were rich merchants of Zanzibar, Mombasa or Dar es Salaam, and it was equally natural that they should give no encouragement to British and Dutch attempts to muscle into the lucrative trade with the Persian Gulf, India and the spice islands of what is now Indonesia. As a result the East African Bantu was exposed to European influence at a later date than the Negroes of Africa's western bulge, and there is little likelihood that he will be ready to control his own political and economic affairs in an efficient manner for many years to come.

Farther to the south, Southern Rhodesia, though vehemently denying anything of the kind, is already politically oriented toward the "race-conscious" Union of South Africa. Uganda and Tanganyika are in a state of flux; Kenya is in turmoil. Back in London the federation of Northern Rhodesia, Southern Rhodesia and Nyasaland has been pushed through by a British government which, on this particular issue, seems to be stone deaf to liberal warnings at home and highly critical opinions abroad. In South Africa the general elections of April 1953 sent Doctor Malan's nationalist extremists, with their white supremacy theories, back to power with an increased majority.

The affairs of the other colonial powers are less complex. So far Belgium has cleverly avoided committing herself to any declared policy on the future status of her colony, emphasizing that the most immediate need is the enactment of widespread social legislation: political education is a secondary consideration which will be put on the curriculum later. The new laws are very successfully aimed at improving the material lot of the inhabitants of the Congo and, though they are used as a smoke screen when the future is brought up for discussion, they are defended by the Belgian authorities with some very sound logic based on a knowledge of the limitations of the Congolese in his present stage of evolution. Thus, in the Belgian Congo benevolent paternalism has taken the place of political orientation, and though the average Congolese may be sleek and well-fed, he doesn't know Karl Marx from Senator McCarthy.

The French, wits and philosophers and temperamentally less likely than the British or Belgians to be concerned with creating good or bad impressions, insist that French-held territories are really extensions of metropolitan France. Their indignation when criticisms of the French Union have been given hearings in the United Nations General Assembly and Political Committee has resounded from pole to pole. Yet the French colonies are like fair mansions with empty rooms, and national near-bankruptcy, extending back almost to the end of the First World War, has prevented lawmakers in Paris from keeping abreast of trends in colonial politics. The cloak of French citizenship is offered to members of all races and creeds within the French Union: with French citizenship will go a legacy of corruption and bitter political strife. On the better side it can be said that the French scorn the color bar. In the late Félix Eboué, a West Indian Negro, French Equatorial Africa had a very capable and widely loved governor-general, but on the seamier side of this absence of discrimination it has to be noted that our Gallic friends are generally unperturbed by the sociological, to say nothing of the moral, issues of unlimited white-black cohabitation.

The Portuguese, too, are little concerned with this latter question. They accept the mulatto socially, and a large number of rich and esteemed Portuguese colonials have Negro blood. The great trouble in Portugal's rich colonies of Angola and Mozambique is that the colonist so often sinks to native level. This applies especially in bush stations, in jungle clearings where one or two Portuguese males with a host of half-breed children run trading posts which net them fortunes they are unable to put to good use. The Portuguese government has made a belated start in Africa, and the Portuguese colonial system as a clear-cut philosophy defies definition. This is only to be expected from a country which has had interminable difficulties with its own political evolution.

Generally, however, the Portuguese employ a despotism, the benevolence of which varies with the expediency of the moment.

The time is fast coming when the embarrassments of the colonial powers must cease to be their private problems. Central Africa is having an industrial revolution over one hundred years later than the countries in whose hands its destiny has so far lain. The African is bewildered and groping; in the space of a few years he has seen agriculture mechanized, young folk drift to the factories or the mines, witch doctors' sons turn into white-coated medical assistants. The incantation has made way for the prescription, the scalpel and the hypodermic syringe.

If these new wonders do not bring an all-round betterment of his lot, the African may become an easy prey to subversive whispers, no matter from what direction they may come. And for this very reason Central Africa could lie right in the path of the Communist bulldozer; the Moscow-trained agitator, like a land surveyor, has already planted his pegs in the valleys and on the hilltops. Genuine collaboration among all the free nations is essential if the very delicate moments ahead are to be turned to peaceful account.

The trickiness of the situation is heightened by the fact that the white man is in Africa to stay. The administrators and other shapers of Africa's future may eventually retire to *honoris causa* professorships. They are the guiding hands which will be withdrawn when the infant is able to walk alone. But complete European withdrawal is neither possible nor desirable. Many white families know only Africa as home. Too much money has been invested, and such strides are being made in tropical hygiene that living and working in Africa have few physical disadvantages nowadays.

A state of peaceful coexistence must be achieved. In order to bring this about a clear and disinterested policy has to be framed in which the colonial powers can themselves assume the leading roles, yet at the same time be bound by their responsibilities to the entire noncommunist world. But I do not see how the colonial powers can shoulder the burden unaided, and intervention, even though it be confined to advice, or at the most to financial assistance, will almost certainly cause resentment because of real or imagined losses of sovereignty and inevitable further sacrifices on already over-strained economies. It may help to point to the achievements of the United Nations Trusteeship Council which redistributed Mussolini's former East African Empire and brought about the federation of Ethiopia and Eritrea. Similar efforts could surely be applied to other colonial problems and could be welcomed by the colonial powers without loss of face.

2

The Congo

THE SECOND of my two long spells in Africa
began and ended in Leopoldville. In the Belgian Congo
I was in constant close touch with members of the colonial administration; as a member of the press bureau I
had a *coupe-file*, a sort of right of entry to all public and
most private functions held in the capital. The notes and
impressions built up from these meetings are the under-
pinnings of my story, since whenever I think of my wider
travels, or get messages telling me of the latest happenings
in other parts of Africa, I relate my thoughts to my much
more comprehensive and recent knowledge of the Belgian Congo and its government. The other African
countries, apart from French Equatorial Africa, I knew
more intimately some years ago, and some of them I saw
only during the last war. I do not say this because I feel
that having seen a country only in wartime invalidates
any of my findings, for, after all, many countries are still
living under wartime economies. I bring up the point,

though, because tourists who have made a recent series of one-day or often only overnight visits to African "places of interest" have said to me, "Oh, but of course, if you were only there in wartime you didn't see the *real* country." Nothing exasperates me more than to hear this; it is untrue, downright poppycock. The life of the people goes on in any country in spite of wars, plagues and famines.

I have developed a fixed habit of relating my more general knowledge of other African countries to my close and sympathetic knowledge and, I hope, understanding of the Belgian Congo. For the African problem is basically the same, no matter what circumstances apply in any given country. Our Odyssey begins, then, in government circles in Leopoldville.

The Atlantic Coast of the Belgian Congo is a mere twenty miles long and lies entirely to the north of the Congo estuary. On the south side lies the Portuguese colony of Angola, while farther to the north are the little Portuguese enclave of Cabinda and the coast of French Equatorial Africa. From the coast the Congo channel runs northeast in a wide sweep and divides into two forks: the Ubangi-Mbomu which continues as the border with French territory up to the frontier of the Sudan, and the main Congo, or Lualaba as it later becomes, which turns southeast through Stanleyville and thence to the rich copper lands of the south. Here lies Northern Rhodesia, while far to the north are the British territories of Tanganyika, Kenya and Uganda, which roll down to the

Indian Ocean from the great lakes of Africa and the hallowed Mountains of the Moon. This vast expanse is all essentially the basin of the Congo. The network of its tributaries drains the whole country, the cities of the Belgian Congo lie on its banks and its broad waters carry a never-ending procession of river traffic which penetrates into the reaches of the Kasai, the Sankuru, the Kwango and the Uele.

While the race for African colonies was going on, Belgium's great imperialist, Leopold II, determined that his country should share in the African spoils. In the middle of August 1879 the first Belgian expedition, led by Henry Morton Stanley, who had entered King Leopold's service, reached the Congo and established a post at Vivi on the northern bank of the river, facing what is now Matadi. In 1881 a steamer service was put into operation between Banana Point on the west coast and Stanley Falls on the Lualaba, about 1,600 miles beyond Leopoldville.

The rapid success of this purely Belgian initiative could not long escape the notice of the other powers in the colonial race. The blue flag with the golden star, the flag of Leopold's International Congo Association, was soon floating over a large number of trading posts in the jungle. In Europe the situation was delicate. The older powers looked askance at the success of the newcomer in their midst. France would only consent to a Belgian annexation of the Congo basin if she were given preferential treatment in matters of trade. After an age of inertia, Portugal suddenly decided to make a stand on her historic position in the western basin of the Congo. Britain tended to support Portugal.

However, General Sanford, the United States Minister in Brussels, took up the task of presenting Belgium's claims in Washington, and in 1884 he returned to Brussels bearing documents signed in the name of President Arthur. Under authority of these papers, the American government gave orders to its officials to recognize the flag of the International Congo Association as the flag of a friendly power. Other nations followed suit and on February 12, 1885, Colonel Strauch, the Belgian spokesman, was able to inform the assembled delegates of the other European powers of the political recognition granted to the new Congo state. Leopold's private association thus assumed the rights of sovereignty. In the following year the Congo Free State was proclaimed and in August 1886 Leopold II, King of the Belgians, added to his titles that of King of the newly created empire.

In 1889 Leopold II made his will. The Congo Free State, which was virtually his personal domain, was to be bequeathed to the Kingdom of Belgium at his death.

It seems to me significant that prior to this there had been very little international comment on Belgium's penetration in the Congo. There had of course been a great deal of speculation as to what Leopold's ultimate achievement would be and to what extent the king's private purse was benefiting from his direct sponsorship of the work of the pioneers. But his diplomatic triumph stung the powers into howls of protest. British merchants who had been unresponsive when Stanley implored them

to put money into a Congo venture now woke up to
what they had missed. Bismarck was furious that this
fait accompli should stand in his way to the domination
of Africa. Portugal, which had for 300 years held a fa-
vorable position on the west coast but had achieved little,
suddenly decided to feel badly done by. It made no
difference.

This shock to the complacency of the great powers did
have an effect in that it produced one of the greatest
smear campaigns in history. In an effort to save face by
a display of indignation which should have deceived
nobody, the European states began a campaign of slander
against the administration of the Congo. Highly colored
atrocity stories appeared in the press; there were tales of
unscrupulous and bloody exploitation; there were even
hints that Leopold was conniving with the Arabs for the
maintenance of the slave trade.

Behind this hullabaloo there were uneasy self-search-
ings in many countries over the administration of their
own colonies. The consciences of the nations were
demanding a cleanup; demands for reform must be publicized. Too much throwing of mud into one another's
gardens might have led to serious international incidents,
but in Belgium—a state whose neutrality had been guaranteed by the powers when this little kingdom was
separated from the Netherlands in 1831—they had a
tailored-to-measure whipping boy.

Atrocities in the Congo there must have been, just as
there must have been similar irregularities in other countries; but we cannot saddle Leopold or the Belgian people

as a whole with the entire blame. To begin with, bloodshed is bound to occur in the pioneer's reduction of obstacles to his progress. There must have been exploitation; it was part of the pattern of the age. But any suggestion that a peculiar capacity for cruelty and desecration was one of the talents of Leopold and his people is quite untenable, even allowing that the nineteenth century was not a kind century, any more than is the twentieth. Furthermore, Belgians, the kindliest of people anyway, were in a minority in the Congo in those days.

The anti-Leopold campaign continued without a sign of letting up until, in 1904, King Leopold declared his willingness to open his dominions to a neutral and impartial committee of investigation. The committee's findings bore out some of the charges, as indeed they were bound to do, and in 1906 a number of reform measures were enacted. From that time the affairs of the Belgian Congo have moved steadily ahead through two world wars; the country is now cruising along the highroad of great material prosperity.

The Belgian writer and poet, Henri Drum—his real name is Van Herreweghe—is a wise, tolerant and understanding man. An *administrateur territorial* of the Belgian Colonial Service, an African linguist with a shrewd insight into the native mind, he is responsible for educating the Congolese by radio. Many Africans now own radio sets, and even in the villages in the bush there is usually some sort of equipment around which listening groups can be organized. Belgium's message to the native

in five Bantu languages can be heard nightly throughout
the Congo basin; it is a poetically conceived, simple little
message in song and parable, full of the colorful allegories
so dear to the African mind. Who could be better fitted
for this mission than a man with poetry in his soul?

I first met Henri Drum on the pilgrimage to 'Mbé. He
is a man past middle age, and I remember how, with a
tight-fitting French beret on the back of his head and a
foul pipe filled with Belgian-grown Semois tobacco
clamped between his teeth, he sat quietly in the back of
the uncomfortable old truck reflecting, so he told me a
long time afterward, on the pessimism of the book of
Ecclesiastes.

Henri, along with Jean-Marie, was a regular client
Chez Armand. In a way he became my guide and mentor: he taught me positively where Jean-Marie taught me
in a negative way with witty cynicisms. In his unusually
slow but dignified, authoritative French, Henri Drum
guided me through the intricacies of the Belgian Ten-
Year Plan for colonial development. This scheme, loudly
acclaimed in the Brussels papers and written up in the
United States and elsewhere, is inevitably discussed in
places where men forgather in Belgium or the Congo.
For *Le Plan décennal* is an embodiment of Belgium's
colonial creed; it is a back cloth on which an appreciation
of life in her colony and an understanding of her aims
can be limned.

Belgium's domestic politics are the source of many
bitter arguments. The country is bilingual, biracial and
sharply divided between the followers of the two main

political parties, the Christian Social party (Catholics) and the Socialists. On the broadest lines the Flemish, Nederlands-speaking element of the population is Catholic, while the French-speaking Walloons make up the greater part of the Socialists. In this necessary oversimplification the Catholics are royalist and traditionalist, but have recently adopted lines of thought which embrace many of the better aspects of liberalism. Since the Socialists are anti-Catholic above all else—*á bas la calotte*— it follows that they are for the most part republicans and freethinkers. This is quite in keeping with the French attitudes of mind of the Walloons, many of whom, as Francophiles, look to Paris as their spiritual home. Moreover the Walloon country has known industrial depression and the ravages of war and has consequently proved a fertile soil for Socialist and Communist propagandists. On the other hand the Flemish area to the north and along the coast—fondly, but mistakenly, imagined by foreigners to be a land of clogs and windmills—is commercial and agricultural and much more conservative.

The two parties are of almost equal strength, and a great deal of redundancy is caused by the necessity of balancing Catholic against non-Catholic in key posts, particularly in the radio and propaganda services. This has understandably led to political finagling in both Belgium and her colony; yet despite these small irregularities Belgium can be proud of her political maturity and her enviable record of stable government.

This evidence of social responsibility is reflected in the Belgian Congo where Walloon industriousness and imagination have combined with the Flemish bourgeois virtues of stolidity, honesty and business acumen to produce a colony which, from the economic standpoint at any rate, is the envy of her colonial neighbors.

This economic prosperity in the Belgian Congo has led many folk, not all of them Belgians, into thinking that the Belgians have a perfect colonial system and that it can continue indefinitely in spite of what is said about the white man's eventually having to relinquish his leadership in Africa. Yet there is an inherent weakness which is often overlooked. It is true that the native is slowly being given more responsibility, but only very slowly, and the Belgian authorities are devoting great attention to the physical and material well-being of the African while giving little encouragement to his nascent political aspirations. Thus the Congolese is less politically conscious than his brother in the French and British colonies, and this constitutes a danger in itself. Honest misinformation, the truth, or deliberate misrepresentation are all swallowed with equal avidity by that section of the native population which realizes that there is something afoot which it is not encouraged to think about.

It is at this point that the smoke screen goes up. The Belgian, whether a Walloon or a Fleming, possesses many of the attributes of leadership. He is a realist, has no use for sentimentality and can be excused, in view of his country's checkered historical background, for having a profound strain of cynicism in his make-up. Questioned on this aspect of Belgium's colonial policy, my Belgian friends—and I have questioned many—have all insisted that the Congolese has to have a full stomach before he can think with any clarity on the problems of his political future. I reply that when he has a full stomach, he will be less likely to worry about his politics—is that what the Belgians want? Suppose, God forbid, some catastrophe overtook Belgium; would not the Congolese be left as intellectually defenseless as the ancient Britons were left militarily defenseless when the Roman legions were suddenly withdrawn? And, in any case, at what future time do you visualize the beginning of the era of the full belly?

The answer is always the same. Well, says the Belgian, we must see how things are when the Ten-Year Plan is completed.

In the meantime it is perfectly true that the Congolese is being provided with opportunities to become a skilled and competent workman. Here is an excellent labor force to be nursed along; the native worker is better housed, clothed, fed and paid than his Bantu cousins in other territories. The promoters know well that their eventual dividends depend on Congolese reactions to this type of European sponsorship, and care is being taken that these reactions are not conditioned by a rapid growth of political consciousness.

On the other hand the Belgian can point in apparent justification of his point of view to the tragic events in Kenya and the political unrest and strikes in the copper belt of Northern Rhodesia. I have succeeded in convincing very few that they may be merely postponing the evil day.

The Ten-Year Plan itself is a bold and imaginative approach to the problems of economic development. "Slow democratization"—the British philosophy—is excluded from its provisions. The planners see that the new economic, political and strategic importance of the Belgian Congo will lead to the quick transformation of the colony from a source of raw materials into an industrial country in its own right.

At the inception of the plan in 1949 there were only about 50,000 white people in the Congo, of whom by far the greatest number were Belgians. There are considerable numbers of Portuguese, mainly traders and plantation operators, among them some of the richest merchants in the country. Likewise there is a fair sprinkling of Greeks, shrewd businessmen whose fathers followed the ancient trading routes from their homeland through Egypt, the Sudan and Uganda to the Congo and South Africa. In the larger cities and out on the vast Lever Brothers' plantations there are British and Americans. There are sizable groups of French and Dutch.

King Leopold II, Belgium's colonizing monarch, guaranteed that the Congo should remain open to any worthy enterprise. In Leopoldville alone I can think of Belgian, Dutch, Portuguese and British companies which distribute automobiles, trucks and automotive equipment. The better-class book trade is in the hands of a Frenchman. There are Armenian dentists, Greek leather merchants, an Italian glass factory and a Swedish import-export corporation. The largest department store is run by enterprising Rhodian Jews. And quite aside from these private concerns such world-wide organizations as Shell, Standard Oil, Texaco, Goodyear and Dunlop are solidly established. Business propositions are given careful consideration by commercial attachés at the consulates of twenty-two different countries.

The door is still open, but its hinges are stiff. During the entire ten years of the project it is proposed to increase the white population from 50,000 to only 80,000 or 90,000, and newcomers will be carefully screened by the Belgian authorities. Rightly so, for the "exploiter" mentality still exists in many would-be immigrants, and there is still that tendency to take out whatever can be taken out of the country and to put back nothing. Among the present colonists there are far too many who dream only of the day when they will have accumulated enough wealth to get out and settle down in Brussels, Antwerp, the Belgian Ardennes, or maybe Lisbon or Athens. A recent good omen, however, is that more retired settlers are remaining in Central Africa. A new generation of young folk is growing up. African-born, African-educated, with little or no knowledge of Europe, they see Africa as their home. Here we have a nucleus. The white African citizen is an essential factor in the future stability of the continent, and this nucleus is being added to under the immigration provisions of the Ten-Year Plan.

Back in 1950 I was told by a Belgian colonial official that the pattern of the white population would change visibly during the next ten years. When I left Leopoldville in 1952 I was beginning to see what he meant. In 1947 the colonial sun helmet of the Belgian civil servant with its gilded badge catching the rays of the sun seemed to be everywhere. The white population seemed to be top-heavy with government employees. This is not so obvious today because the emphasis has already begun to move away from the imported administrator to the imported businessman, industrialist or planter. The change is not due to any drastic streamlining of the Colonial Service; it is simply that the lower grades are slowly being filled by Congolese. As clerical assistants on routine business Africans are painstaking and can generally be relied on to make no grave errors, but my experience of them in government, banking and other business has established that they are still in constant need of supervision. For all that, the native is slowly moving up the nonexecutive grades in government and business; the lower-grade white clerk is moving out, and the immigration trend toward the independent colonist continues.

I have spent many hours with Belgians discussing the question of why they propose only to double the white population of the Congo by 1959. Is it, I ask, because you feel that the country is not yet ready to absorb even this small number over the prescribed period? Is it because you think it would be bad for Belgian morale if you couldn't get any more than forty to fifty thousand newcomers no matter what inducements you offered? Or is it because immigration seems to have little appeal to other groups than workers and businessmen, and you are afraid of upsetting the intellectual balance?

It is in fact noticeable that the Congo attracts very few intellectuals aside from those who have come to work among the natives. I broached this question to a colleague in Brussels. He said, "*Mais, qu'est ce que tu veux? Y'a pas de vie intellectuelle là bas.*" In other words, there was no outlet for his intellectual proclivities in the Congo. In a sense he was right, for the musical societies and the art and literary groups in Congolese cities do have a decidedly provincial flavor, but they work on a much higher plane than the Belgian public imagines. In this sphere the *Bruxellois* regards the Congo in much the same light as the Bostonian sees Iowa or the Dakotas. But since intellectuals are so prone to adopt "fads," it would not surprise me to find many of them flocking down to the Congo in the next few years to worship at the shrine of the new "neo-primitive-expressionist" indigenous literature and painting.

The Belgian reply to these queries is that the authorities are not in favor of unlimited immigration into the Congo for a variety of reasons. They want settlers to carve out their own niches and not to compete for those already filled. They want to ensure that the ratio of Belgians to other Europeans will not be depressed. I can sympathize with this latter point, since the average Belgian, whether townsman or peasant, is happy and prosperous and generally unwilling to leave his homeland. Unlimited immigration would certainly lead to an influx of settlers from the less favored lands of southern Europe.

In the case of the businessman immigrant, there is no real problem. He has money to invest, and in ninety-nine cases out of a hundred he will have had some experience with the African trade. There is, however, a crucial need for white artisans, but these are not forthcoming, largely, I suspect, because the notion that it would give the natives ideas of equality to see Europeans working with their hands is still prevalent, though slowly dying. The Ten-Year Plan urges that colonists are needed who are not afraid of manual labor. If a man is going to execute a government contract, he is expected to roll up his sleeves and himself take over the job of personal supervision instead, as is not uncommon, of hiring an inefficient native foreman.

White farmers and soil-conservation experts are badly needed, not only in the Belgian Congo but in most parts of the continent, for the African left to himself is a spasmodic and wasteful cultivator. It is in this sphere that the best terms are being offered; the agricultural colonist is to be given a long-term loan up to twenty years, and his land is to be surveyed and partially cleared by the government. Yet I do not find it surprising that the response is slow. The newcomers may or may not have been farm workers in their own country, and there have been many whose first experience of African farming has been startling and maybe a little disheartening: crops of which they know little, a constant fight against the encroaching bush, the worries of dealing with willing, though exasperatingly dense, native help. Fears that movements similar to Mau Mau will spread over the continent act as an additional deterrent.

Farming in Africa can be made to pay, and pay well. Experimental stations adduce daily proof that certain European crops can be grown successfully, and indigenous strains are being developed by scientific methods. Maybe there will be more encouraging signs in the next few years for there are acres upon acres of good land going for the asking.

The specific provisions of the Ten-Year Plan are interesting. Mining, the mainstay of the Congo's economy, has priority over other projects, since by 1949 most of the surface and shallow deposits of metallic ores had been exploited. Some plans for underground operations would have had to be worked out whether there was a Ten-Year Plan or not, so the general scheme has been framed to include the mechanization of the mining industry and the modernization of associated projects.

The Belgian Congo is by far the world's greatest producer of industrial diamonds, and the 1949 output of 9,000,000 carats is to be increased to 13,000,000 by the end of the decade. The output of jewelry diamonds is expected to stay around 700,000 carats, but fine gold production, which was over fourteen tons in 1949, is planned to average sixteen tons per annum from now on. Copper production is to be stepped up to over 180,000 tons, and there are hopes that the deeper diggings will bring about a substantial increase on the 1951 figure of 16,000 tons of tin and the tin-bearing ore, cassiterite. As far back as 1946 the Belgian Congo was producing 7,000,000 pounds of cobalt and cobaltiferous ores, as against 1,000,000, just over 600,000 and 100,000 pounds in Northern Rhodesia, French Morocco and Canada, respectively, the next largest producers; this gap should be widened under the plan's provisions, which call for an increase of up to twenty-five per cent. No figures are obtainable for uranium, though it is estimated that the Congo has some 80 per cent of the world's known deposits—outside the Iron Curtain countries. Furthermore, Congo uranium ores are of very high quality, and without them, as Mr. Gordon Dean admitted early in 1953, the United States would be hard put to complete its atomic-energy program. Of the other metals silver, manganese, zinc, tantalum, niobium, wolfram, platinum, palladium and cadmium, as well as a wide variety of precious and semiprecious stones, can be produced to cope with market demands.

The present coal output of the Belgian Congo is low, some 60,000 tons a year. Numerous rich deposits have been located, but so far they have not been exploited industrially on any large scale, mainly because of transportation difficulties. The principal use of coal in the Congo at present is as a flux in copper smelting, and no startling production increase is planned.

The hydroelectric schemes in the colony rank among the most ambitious in the world; plans for an intensive harnessing of the Congo waters have been in operation for years and are still developing rapidly.

In view of the importance of the Congo's mining industry, the labor force employed is small: 150,000 African workers and 2,500 European technicians keep the entire enterprise going. In 1951 the *African World* stated that, if anything, this force would tend to decrease in numbers owing to large-scale mechanization and because in any case it is not the policy of the Belgians to attract more and more Africans to the mines. They prefer to see a return of the native to the agricultural life and are making this means of existence more pleasant by the introduction of modern farming methods, which should lead to an improvement in native husbandry, and by the provision of adequate medical services, housing, drinking water and clothing. Over $20,000,000 have been earmarked for native housing; the water supply is to be tripled and the yearly amount of clothing material available to each African is to be increased from four yards to about sixteen yards, based on the estimated requirements for Indonesia and India.

The vast new health program is very much in keeping with Belgium's conception of colonial development. This does not mean to imply that the Belgian health scheme is infinitely ahead of plans in operation in other African countries, but certainly the document is an ambitious one and emphasizes the Belgian preoccupation with the material well-being of the Congolese. Belgian doctors and surgeons have always been renowned for their skill and enterprise, and the medical history of the Congo shows great progress from the very beginning. At the opening of the century there were only thirty doctors and one pharmacist in the entire territory. By 1947 the number had risen to 377 doctors, twenty-seven pharmacists and eighteen dentists, while at the present moment there are well over 700 in the medical service, to say nothing of thousands of nurses, native and white medical assistants, native orderlies and a well-staffed department of hygiene. The Ten-Year Plan calls for an increase of 144 per cent on the present establishment, the setting up of twenty-nine new medical centers—each with two fully equipped hospitals, one for natives and one for Europeans—new laboratories, rural dispensaries, a tuberculosis sanatorium and several mental hospitals.

For the first time the Congo is to have two *centres universitaires*, which will cater to students from all over the country. Teaching will be in French—the language all the students will have in common—and the bent will be practical with improved facilities for training Africans in the various vocations at present open to them.

The most efficient way of getting around this part of Africa is by air. The entire Congo basin has a well-developed air network; there are almost 200 airfields in the Belgian Congo and services to Europe and America are assured by some of the world's major air lines. But once out of the air and on the ground the traveler finds himself in a quandary. The rail network is poor; roads are still practically nonexistent except in the towns. River transport is the easiest and cheapest means of travel, but it is slow. These deficient lines of communication are hampering the country's industrial development; the almost unlimited industrial potential is in danger of being bogged down by shortage of transportation facilities. In the entire country there are at present only 72,000 miles of roads, and for the most part these are morasses in the eight-month wet season and slippery sand in the dry weather. Five axial routes are planned, and these are to be served by a number of feeder roads. The axial roads and their feeders are already in existence for the most part, though in places they are little better than jungle trails. But the great-grandfathers of the natives who will be working on the new highways hewed out these trails by constant experiment; as a result the surveyor knows roughly where to take his theodolite, and the new road map, except for the addition of 8,000 miles of new cuttings, will be substantially the same as before. The difference will be that the 1959 roads will be motorable: they should be, for over $125,000,000 will have been spent on them.

The most-used method of transport in the Congo is now, and will be for some years, the river-railroad combination; yet only one new railroad is contemplated and it will be a mere 280 miles long. The new line, which will be laid in the extreme east of the Congo, will connect the Katanga line with the Great Lakes Railway and will be on the South African gauge. The adoption of this slightly wider gauge, 1.067 meters as against one meter, will complete rail-river connections from Matadi in the west to Dar es Salaam in Tanganyika. The vital Leopoldville-Matadi line is to be electrified.

Old Man River is certainly not being forgotten. Forty million dollars are to be spent on the deep-sea ports of Matadi, Boma and Banana, the pilot station on the South Atlantic coast, and the inland ports of Leopoldville, Stanleyville and secondary points between. Navigation channels are to be improved and extensive use is already being made of radar to guide the river steamers through the sandbanks.

The Ten-Year Plan is now well under way, though it

had some serious teething pains in 1952. The tremendous increase in imports and exports caused a transport crisis which threatened to bring much of the work to a standstill. At one time I remember the situation was so grave that the authorities of the port of Matadi absolutely forbade all imports for several weeks. The Leopoldville-Matadi railway could not cope with the backlog on the quaysides; the river fleet could not handle the increased volume of inland traffic. The two bottlenecks were gradually cleared, but only a maintenance of the present phenomenal effort will prevent a recurrence of the predicament. There are no means of by-passing river transport when sending goods upcountry, for no railroad leads east from Leopoldville and the road which leads south and east is certainly not capable of carrying heavy truck traffic.

As it is elsewhere, the labor shortage is one of the Congo's greatest problems. At the beginning of 1952 nearly 1,000,000 natives—that is to say about thirty-five per cent of the adult male population—were employed on one development project or another. Of these, 780,000 came from the villages. It may be true that there is still a great labor force untapped in the bush, but the Belgian authorities have warned that too much faith must not be put in this possibility for medical, agricultural and social reasons. Some equilibrium, they assert, must be maintained between the rural villages and the industrial non-tribal communities; and if labor continues to be recruited from the Congolese peasantry, this balance will disappear and with it will disappear a good proportion of the food supplies these cultivators produce. The fight to preserve the balance is a losing one, and it has already been found necessary to import food for the native populations of the cities. The problem has not yet reached serious dimensions—it was pointed out in 1952 that if the daily ration of the city worker were to be fixed at 250 grams, or nine ounces, of wheat flour per day, then Leopoldville's quarter of a million or more Africans could be fed on the cargoes of only two large freighters a year. By increasing wheat-flour deliveries from abroad it would be possible to take more Congolese peasants from their present occupations and use them in the various development schemes, and it is argued in favor of this means of approaching the problem that the price of foodstuffs could be more easily stabilized and the purchasing power of the African's wages be increased.

A more obvious remedy for the labor shortage would be to make a less wasteful use of the labor available and to increase the efficiency of the worker by granting increased facilities for professional and technical training. According to Monsieur Cornélis, the Director General of Economic Affairs in the Belgian Congo, ten per cent of the present labor force could be saved by rationalizing methods of work. Monsieur Cornélis favors more widespread mechanization, giving as an example the present methods of coffee sorting. The sorting of 20,000 tons of coffee a year requires 1,000,000 working days involving the continued presence of 5,000 natives. The mechanical sorting of this amount would require only ten native workers and two European technicians.

Although the bulldozer is much more in evidence than it was when I arrived in the Congo in 1947, excessive numbers of natives are still being employed on road-paving projects—a wasteful way of absorbing the drifters who make their way to the towns with no skill of any kind and very little natural adaptability. The African needs very little encouragement to lean on his shovel and fall into a reverie: he wastes a great deal of time working with his mouth, and a gang of native laborers can be heard chattering within a radius of hundreds of yards. Small wonder the quality of work is inferior.

The Belgian Congo's Ten-Year Plan has six years to go; therefore its eventual success is still a matter for speculation. So far the scheme is working out unaccompanied by the economic misery and political upheavals which have been the results of industrial revolutions in other countries.

3

Leopoldville

LEOPOLDVILLE began as many another city before it, a few fragile huts on a sandy bluff. But, unlike Rome, it was built in a day, or little longer. Some cities take centuries to reach greatness; the capital of the Belgian Congo has reached it in three generations. The three native villages of Ndolo, Kinshasa and Kinsuka have lost their identities and made way for a city which now stretches more than seven miles along the left bank of the Congo. A population which could a short time ago be counted in the hundreds has now stretched to more than a quarter of a million, and there is no easing off in sight. Leopoldville is the largest and richest city between Cairo and Johannesburg, its pulse is loud and heavy: it has that big-city feel.

The transition from reed-thatched hut to skyscraper has taken place since Leopold II of the Belgians joined the nineteenth-century race for colonies and grabbed the million-square-mile Congo basin for his personal domain.

It was not until after the explorer Stanley passed by in 1877 that the first river steamboat—a Mississippi veteran, dismantled, brought from America and reassembled— made its appearance on Stanley Pool, a broad swelling of the Congo's channel just above where Leopoldville now stands. It is as only yesterday that the same Stanley, referring to the rapids which prevent the workers in the Congo hinterland from sending their produce by river down to the sea, said to Leopold II: "Sire, without a railway your empire will not be worth a penny." At the turn of the century native porters and dromedaries were laboring under burdens now rushed along the concrete highways of the city in modern trucks: there was no stagecoach-and-wagon phase. There were no stores, no churches, no restaurants, nor even wayside chophouses. There was a year-round reception committee of flies, mosquitoes, wildcats, boa constrictors and crocodiles, bringing sleeping sickness, malaria, blood poisoning, crushed and maimed limbs and, not infrequently, death itself.

That was Leopoldville when Joseph Conrad, for a time a Congo river pilot, saw on the bluffs overlooking the river a party of whites—drawn, pale, listless shadows of Europeans. Those were the pioneers whose last resting place is a little cemetery dotted with sad leaning crosses, a graveyard of coarse creeping grass on a hill above the old town. Belgians were by no means in the majority in those early wide-open days: the names on the monuments tell us that the newcomers were from the Low Countries, France, Britain, America, Sweden, Italy,

Germany. What the inscriptions do not tell us is that among them were adventurers, missionaries, rogues, vagabonds and soldiers of fortune like Kalina, a swash-buckling Hungarian cavalry officer in the early Congo defense force who went to a spectacular but foolhardy death when he tried to jump on horseback from the cliff to a boat which was sailing by in the swirling brown waters forty feet below.

The City above the Rapids lies on a curve of the river, and behind the bustling quays and marshaling yards its houses, shops, hotels and factories flood the plain, almost to the foothills of the low mountain barrier on the southern horizon. On what were swamps and muddy inlets stand shipyards, textile mills, warehouses, oil and petroleum storage tanks, palm-oil and soap fac-tories, engineering shops and a huge boot-and-shoe plant. The *kinois*, as Leopoldville residents call themselves, can buy shirts, socks, shoes, Lux soap, leather goods, jewelry, beer and Coca-Cola and know with certainty that these were all manufactured within the city limits.

Towering above the dockland drabness—Leopoldville has as yet no Riverside Drive—is the first skyscraper in Central Africa. There are others in the city now, but the Forescom Building, visible for miles, has become the symbol of the new city. The Forescom and other tall buildings standing against the blue African sky give the impression that they do not altogether belong: they are blatant, precocious, a source of wonder, and not in any way part of the Africa of the travelogues. The tourist, conditioned by voices which purport to speak for the globe, finds that the city has an aggressive newness; every building, every shop sign, seems bold and brassy. The streets are jammed with late-model American, British, French and Italian automobiles and trucks. The public transport system uses German *Volkswagens*. A noisy marshaling yard with groaning diesels and shrieking steam locomotives lies right under the balconies of those guests of the Palace Hotel who have succeeded in getting rooms overlooking the river.

Yet in the older suburbs something of the Africa of the early settlers remains. Westward toward Kinsuka and along the dusty road to Kasangulu are bungalows with wide screened porches on all four sides, set in clusters of mango, flamboyant, jacquaranda and palm trees. There are hedges of crimson and purple bougain-villaea, honeysuckle, hibiscus, bamboo, poinsettia and cactus of a dozen kinds, while in the garden grow pine-apple, papaw, avocado pear, tomatoes, cucumbers, sweet corn and sometimes limes, oranges and grapefruit. Here the traffic moves more slowly and in the heat of the day when the garden boy's scythe swishes lazily to the ac-companiment of a chorus of bees, it seems a lotus land, always afternoon.

Across the river, Brazzaville, capital of French Equa-torial Africa, swelters in the blazing sun. A slim white obelisk and the governor's mansion shimmer in the heat haze which shrouds the cliff above the river narrows. As the eye sweeps eastward past Brazzaville docks, island-strewn Stanley Pool stretches out into the distance. Far beyond, in the amethyst haze, can be seen the Crystal

Mountains, once believed to hold rich mineral ores. The guess was wrong, and the Crystal Mountains slumber on, unscarred by the picks and shovels of the miners. This is the kind of soft beauty which holds more appeal for me than all your Ruwenzoris and Kilimanjaros. I used to like nothing better than to drift gently among the palm-clad islands, remembering, speculating and waiting for the world to change with the dying sun.

The tropical nights can outdo the lazy afternoons in charm. They are warm, moon-kissed, voluptuous, sub-tle. As the sun sets, the white buildings diffuse a pinkish, coral glow, which makes the African twilights as beautiful as they are short. The hours of daylight on the equator are the same, give or take twenty minutes, all the year round; and five o'clock, an hour before nightfall, is the hour of metamorphosis. The city comes to life: the streets throng with office and factory workers, the side-walk cafés fill up as hot, thirsty men take their iced beer and wine before moving homeward. Native newsboys run from table to table with the *Courrier d'Afrique* for the Catholics and the *Avenir Coloniale Belge* for the Socialists; for Belgians are inevitably one or the other, and the Flemings and Walloons are almost the equals of the French and the Greeks as tavern oracles. Tall Mos-lems from Nigeria and Senegal set out their stocks of ivoryware, mother-of-pearl, native leatherwork and rugs on the sidewalks outside the hotels and cafés; the neons flash and the cars purr by. Making their way toward the native city are thousands of Africans in buses, on cycles, or on foot, singing and shouting as they go.

In the *Belge*, the segregated native city, live well over 250,000 Africans. Matriarchal systems notwithstanding, the women do most of the heavy chores, and the descending eventide gives birth to a hustle-bustle as housewives with glass demijohns on their heads move toward the public drinking fountains for their water supply. There they queue up patiently, gossiping loudly—the African tongue is quieted only by sleep and death—admiring one another's clothes. Some are wearing European dresses, but by far the greater proportion of the women wear long *pagnes*, robes of brightly colored cloth, native in pattern, but manufactured by the mile in the mills of Holland, Belgium and Great Britain. About one woman in three has a baby on her back, slung pickaback fashion in a length of the same material as the *pagne*, while woolly heads are swathed in gay silk turbans, now frequently worn kerchiefwise in imitation of bobby soxers seen in the movies. Very few of these women are fat; they follow no diet, but heavy work—which drives most of them to an early grave—keeps them slim, though somewhat attenuated. The few fat mammas to be seen are the wives of prosperous west-coast African merchants: they have been to "fattening school" before marriage. "Decrimped" hair styles have as yet made little impression in the Congo, and the only ladies who sport them are either *no-ladies* from African dance halls or very beautiful mulatto girls, who, from the time they are fourteen or so, are cast for the role of *femme entretenue*. A gay, noisy throng.

The air is heavy with the spicy smoke of a myriad little

wood fires, and the cloying sweetness of frangipani, an African magnolia with a waxy, deathlike beauty, rides the air. Children in various stages of undress make driving a hazard, while dandies with loud bow ties, horn-rimmed spectacles, zoot suits and purple socks cycle through the crowd with the assurance which is the privilege of the well-dressed. Abomandi Gaspard, the African cabinetmaker, is now putting up his shutters; Miguel Santos, the mulatto photographer—"*Spécialiste en Noces*"—is taking in the display pictures of self-conscious young bloods who have braved the camera's evil eye. In little native stores oil lamps cast a soft glow over peanuts, bread, Coca-Cola, corned beef and canned herring in tomato sauce, while with myopic eyes tailors and alteration hands, with their ubiquitous Singer sewing machines, toil on into the night.

Blaring music begins to seep through the closely set palisade fences of the cafés where the well to do sip their drinks around little wooden tables, hidden from the gaze of the less fortunate. A line of pickaninnies in neat blue print dresses, followed by two kind-faced Flemish nuns bustling like Christmas geese, makes its way from the *école primaire* to the cathedral.

The music blares louder. But it is no longer the music of Africa. The tom-tom has given way to jazz, the ritual dance has become a rumba. The musicians have forsaken their raffia skirts and beads for white shirts, black bow ties and peppermint-candy-striped narrow pantaloons.

Between the native city and the European and business quarters lies a broad green belt cut by the Avenue Baudouin, a broad cement highway joining the two cities. Here is the Leopoldville zoo and the aquarium, where we used to go on Sunday afternoons. Tea at the zoo is a weekly event in Leopoldville's social calendar. It affords a glance at Africa's larger fauna, at the gorillas and chimpanzees, the mangy lions and the leopards who pace restlessly in their cages near the children's playground. For few citizens of Leopoldville will ever see a lion or leopard except in captivity. Like their European and American counterparts they are preoccupied with more mundane things: they have livings to earn in shops, offices and factories.

The city's daily social event is the arrival of the White Train from Matadi. Hundreds of citizens gather at the depot around six o'clock—some to meet friends returning from trips to Matadi or vacations in Europe, others just to gaze in pity or envy at the dusty, weary travelers, a few of whom will stay in Leopoldville, but most of whom will go still farther inland on the next upriver boat.

Toward eight o'clock, when the heat of the day has subsided a very little—the temperature range is rarely more than fifteen degrees in any twenty-four hours—the cinemas open their doors. Night shifts are preparing for work in the shipyards and textile mills; music comes through open doors, and through mosquito screens can be seen family gatherings similar to those in millions of homes all over the world. City life, whether in the Congo or in America, has become standardized. Yet even in Leopoldville something of the old Africa remains. By the water at Ndolo fishing nets are being repaired, women are making crude earthenware pottery, and out on the bosom of the river tall naked men guide their sleek little craft with the skill born of generations of fishermen. In the shadows a tom-tom beats.

Everywhere there are evidences of a peaceable co-existence of black and white. There seems to be a tacit acceptance of the fact that the white man is in Africa for good. But here and there little arguments, puny quarrels, like twanging nerves, used to make me conscious of hidden unrest below the surface of everyday life. To neglect these symptoms would be to court disaster. Yet present white apathy convinces me that a great deal of complacency both in Africa and throughout the world at large will one day be rudely shaken.

As everywhere else nowadays, the cost of living in Leopoldville and throughout the Congo generally is not cheap. Butter and steak are over a dollar a pound; veal is two dollars a pound, a European chicken costs five dollars, fresh milk is twenty-five cents a pint. A European cabbage would cost about sixty cents; onions are seventeen cents and leeks thirty cents a pound. The best vegetables and meat have to be imported by sea or air and this makes them expensive, but modern cattle husbandry has made great strides lately and some good herds are being raised in places where only ten years ago they would have been decimated by sleeping sickness. The island of Mateba, in the Congo estuary, has a profitable experimental herd; and just as the tsetse fly and the mosquito are being overcome and hopes of providing a cheaper domestic meat supply are rising, so it is now being found possible to grow good vegetables on the high ground. Not far from the capital is Thysville, named after a Matadi railroad pioneer, where, at an altitude of three thousand feet, there are flourishing gardens which supply the city markets at most seasons of the year, but more especially between June and October, which is the dry season in the Congo.

Even down in the humid swamplands by the river it is being found possible to raise fair truck gardens by manuring scientifically and erecting sun shelters over the fast-growing plants. The great trouble with these *marais* is that the vegetables have to be picked when they are small. The tropical deluges which come at the rate of one, sometimes two, a week from October to April either wash the seedlings out of the ground or soak them to such an extent that they become pithy.

On the other hand tropical fruits can be had almost for the asking. Tomatoes spread like weeds, papaw trees springing up in the most impoverished soil and even from garbage heaps will produce fruit in six months or less. Mangoes come in what is the fall in northern climates—in countries south of the equator the spring—and are usually to be found in abundance within two or three weeks following the first September showers, locally dubbed the "mango rains." The climate is too wet for date palms to grow, but there are avocados *ad nauseam* and all the citrus fruits. The cornucopia pours forth pineapples, custard apples, mangosteens and bananas, the last-named so plentifully that they are fed to cattle. But there are no apples, grapes, plums or pears unless you are willing to pay anything from forty cents to a dollar a pound.

Though I tried to get by on local produce in the hopes of returning from the tropics a rich uncle, I had to give up the attempt and spend a lot of money on imported meat and vegetables. But I found the high wages paid in the Congo offered some compensation for the cost of living. The average white employee's wage is around $400 a month after deduction of income tax and social-security contributions, and all companies employing Europeans are obliged to house them, or make a cash allowance in lieu of rent, and pay medical expenses, even to hospitalization charges, surgical interventions and maternity cases. Belgian social legislation, which is highly developed under government auspices, applies in the Congo without respect to nationality, status or earnings. Family allowances are paid quarterly. I used to receive $160 every three months for my wife and two children, and since the allowance for each child increases on a sliding scale, families with, say, six or more children have a combined family allowance which is almost as much as the breadwinner's salary. Yet income tax is only a flat rate of ten per cent.

Leopoldville is an all-electric city. There is no coal-gas supply and none envisaged, owing to the difficulty of transporting the coal. Electricity is rather expensive—more expensive, I feel, than it need be—and bills which are basically exorbitant are skyrocketed by native servants who do not seem to realize that if the iron, the oven

and the lights of every room are left switched on, there
will be a heavy bill at the end of the month. Though our
houseboys were considered among the best to be found
we finally had to revert to the charcoal iron, with which
they are very proficient, while for a time we cooked on
a kerosene range—until we found that the consumption
of kerosene was abnormally high!

Household help in the Congo is easy to come by.
There are good cooks, good washboys, good houseboys
who can be trained, at the cost of high blood pressure, as
table waiters, and there is the ubiquitous *moké*, more
often than not a son or nephew of the cook or washboy.
The *moké* shines the shoes, cleans the car, helps with the
washing up in a costly way—china shops do a roaring
business in Africa—and can be bullied by the others into
taking a hand at almost anything. Our *moké* Graçia, a
Portuguese native from Angola, quickly learned to cook
English breakfasts and by the time he moved up to
houseboy, at the age of fourteen, he could iron very
well and was quite a hand at polishing furniture. A
highly polished hard wax coat has to be maintained on
the furniture to prevent a damp "blue film" from forming. Graçia's predecessor, Dominique, who had six
fingers on each hand and never broke a plate, left us to
take a good job. He came back to see us some months
later dressed in a white flannel suit with a blue pin stripe,
patent leather shoes with white vamps, a loud tie and
sideburns. As a gift (Africans always bring gifts when
visiting) he brought us a hand of bananas and some eggs.

On the whole relations between the European or

American housewife in the Congo and her native help are good. There is a certain amount of pilfering, a great deal of feigned sickness—put on because Africans love to dose themselves up with any of the patent medicines on the bathroom shelf—there are a great many hangovers after palm-wine drinking sessions in the native city, and now and then there is a little shirt-ruining by the wash-boy when he needs one of his master's castoffs.

However, we never had serious trouble with any of our boys. Simon, our cook and headboy generally, was with us for five years. He was an excellent cook, an even better laundryman when he had to be, a good furniture polisher, practical plumber and mechanic, and he could control the other houseboys without great difficulty. We had less luck with the houseboys, who tended to go looking for better jobs just when we had finished the chore of training them. We lost one very good boy this way. Simon told me he had managed to get a job through one of his cronies as a steward on the Congo riverboats. *"Il aura des pourboires"*—"He'll get tips," said Simon.

Our Simon was a gem. Unlike the greater proportion of native house servants, he could read and write both his native dialect and French and could have gone far if he had had any ambition. He even learned a little English. I heard him practicing behind the kitchen door one day— "Me go home? Me go home?" The interrogative was nicely controlled, and sure enough, five minutes later he came sidling up to my wife: "Me go home?"

That was one of the few things about Simon which

annoyed us. He would slip off home at nights (African servants in the Congo are not allowed to live in unless their employer's house is a long way from the native city) and we would find that he'd put dirty saucepans back in the cupboard for the *moké*, who left around four o'clock in the afternoon, to wash early the next morning. Simon's excuse was that he wanted to be home before the picket squads were out. There have been some cases of violence in recent years and now, unless they have a signed and dated permit from their employers, Africans found in the European city after nine at night are liable to have a night's free lodging in the jail. To even things up, whites are not tolerated in the native city after dark.

On festive occasions Simon would disappear before it was time to ask me for a pass, and this eagerness to get away was usually a hint that there would be a hangover next morning. One evening about eight-thirty I caught Simon, with the cook from next door and one of the boys from across the way, about to get into a taxi with a four-gallon demijohn of Portuguese wine. This vino, which sells extensively in Central Africa, is very much *vin ordinaire:* it costs a dollar a gallon and carries authority. Since the taxi trip would cost the conspirators at least another dollar, it meant that they were headed for a very special feast. I remember this occasion since, oddly enough, Simon showed up bright and fresh at seven-thirty next morning. He never would tell me where he got the wine, and I hadn't the heart to report the matter although it is illegal in the Congo to sell anything but beer to an African. The African has a weakness for alcohol; if he can't buy standard products he reverts to drinking the palm-wine and banana-beer concoctions with which he has been stupefying himself for ages.

We enjoyed having the boys around quite apart from any work they did. Africans all have a great sense of fun: they laugh easily and love to play children's games. They adore children and will spoil them completely if a brake is not applied. Simon's greatest pang when we left the Congo was that he wouldn't see his little Janey for a long time, if ever again. We still write to him and he replies in his tolerably good French. His most recent letter, which arrived in November, tells of his purchase of a plot of land near Boma on the Congo estuary and of his difficulties with the labor he has hired to build his new five-room brick house.

The Congo's social legislation applies to the native, too. Simon is married, a staunch Protestant, a solid family man with two delightful little girls, Jeanne and Paulina. His basic wage when working for us was twenty dollars a month. In addition to this he was given two dollars a week for ration money which was used mainly by his family, for he fed frequently on our kitchen. This ration allowance is included in a native's engagement contract, as is a family allowance. The family allowance for a man with two children amounts to ten dollars a month and is paid in fortnightly installments. Thus Simon made altogether thirty-eight dollars a month, and on top of this he received a cut of meat each week end, free tea, coffee, sugar and rice, while he was supplied with, or given the money for, uniforms and work-aprons. I should add that under a tacit agreement he used our soap and hot water for his family wash.

Since Simon, like most Africans, can feed himself on a few cents a day, he is able to save quite a lot of money. His overhead is two dollars a month rent for his house and four dollars a year taxes; these were usually covered by Christmas bonuses and the fare for the mythical railroad trip he made when he took his annual two-weeks' paid vacation.

As proof of his material prosperity Simon—whose surname is Wilson, a name adopted from the minister who baptized his father—has a brightly colored bicycle with dynamo electric lighting and a three-speed contraption set in the hub of the rear wheel. He is the possessor of several European-style suits, a phonograph, a portable battery radio and two wrist watches which he often wears at the same time. His wife and children are always well dressed and very clean. They are included in the free medical schemes, and the little girls go regularly to school, where they are taught to read and write. Later on they will learn something of sewing, embroidery, cookery with modern utensils and other features of housewifery. I found out that until elementary education became completely free, Simon used to pay a small sum each week to cover the cost of teaching materials. He has the right idea, and it is gratifying to see that more and more Africans are doing as Simon does.

It is surprising that in this land of lush plenty the native's diet is drab and uninteresting. He lives on very little meat, a lot of dried fish, manioc flour, rice and bananas; and in spite of preparing European dishes or seeing them prepared, he is very seldom tempted by them. The reason for this drabness is that the African is conservative in matters of food and that few, if any, of the common tropical fruits and vegetables are indigenous to Central Africa. They have all been introduced from abroad, mainly from South America and the Orient during the days of colonial development. I often used to wonder what these people ate before bananas, rice and manioc were grown in Africa. Once I wondered aloud and my guest said: "Each other, possibly." After that I looked carefully at all job applicants to see if they had filed teeth.

How did we entertain ourselves in Africa? The principal game is tennis, but, taking Leopoldville as an average, I find that relaxation and sport follow much the same patterns as they do in the temperate zone. There is the Royal Leopoldville Golf Club, eighteen holes with a top-notch British professional; there are swimming pools, riding schools, a boat club and a *Bal Pelote* league. *Bal Pelote*, a strenuous game which has to be confined to the younger element, is a type of Basque *pelota*. Association football, the national game of Britain and Belgium and adopted by Portugal, is played with great enthusiasm by Europeans and Africans. Some of the African leagues play without boots, and there are surprisingly few broken toes. The temperature doesn't discourage the football fans, and in the hottest of weather games are played at night under floodlights in a stadium which can accommodate 70,000 spectators. For complete relaxation there are clubs and cinemas, and Leopoldville and all the larger cities enjoy frequent visits from European theater companies.

So, you see, life in African cities is much the same as anywhere, except that in Africa there is an institution which spoils returning travelers for working American office hours. The absolute minimum lunch period is two hours: lunch is served at twelve, shutters are drawn and the entire white population retires to bed. The siesta is a blessed idea, and the day does not need to be hot for a siesta to be enjoyed.

Work starts early in the morning; the business of the day is in full swing shortly after seven o'clock. Some offices work straight through from seven until two o'clock in the afternoon and then call it a day; others work from eight to twelve and from two or three o'clock to five in the evening or even later. Outdoor workers, African and European, start at daybreak and carry on until the oppressive heat of midafternoon forces them to capitulate to the sun. What surprises me most of all is that the work gets done in spite of heat and tempest.

4

The River

In this age of transition in Africa the modern rubs cheeks with the primitive at every turn in the road and every bend in the river. On the fringes of the new cities are mud-and-wattle villages. Great estates cultivated by modern machines are bordered by native acreages whose soil has known nothing heavier than the simple hoe. Trains laden with hundreds of tons of freight rumble past files of Africans wending their way to market with bundles of produce on their heads. Dugout canoes bob up and down in the wake of sleek diesel motor vessels.

Wherever I went in Africa there were constant reminders that tomorrow and yesterday, uneasy bedfellows, lie side by side, and nowhere did this become more obvious than at little native settlements just outside the limits of the cities. The first trip I took upriver on the Congo, though a short one of only a few hours, made impressions on me which all subsequent gallivanting has failed to change.

That trip, etched so deeply in my mind, took me to the inhabited island of Bamu, a French territory lying a mile or so from the north shore of Stanley Pool. A haven of birds, butterflies and hill-building termites, Bamu lies low in the water, is surrounded by dense reeds (*matiti* in Lingala) and carries a forest of mango and borassus palms on its gently rounded back. Henri, a young Belgian who knows every channel through the sandbanks, was my host and guide. As we nosed out from the muddy creek where Henri keeps his outboard motorboat, the sky was cloudless and the sun beat down mercilessly. There was hardly a breath of wind as we made our way around clumps of *matiti* and floating islands—Portuguese concessions, as the Belgians call them. We had the river to ourselves; most of the natives around the Pool are night fishermen, and at this time of the afternoon they were resting up for another night's work. A mile out a butterfly flopped lazily by. I had begun to speculate on whether a butterfly could fly a mile or whether it could ride on the surface of the water, when I realized that this particular butterfly had probably come down with one of these small islands which are broken off the riverbanks by storms upcountry and float downstream for miles until they are dashed to pieces on the rapids.

On we went past stilt villages planted in a wilderness of reeds. The poles which support the huts are driven deep through the *matiti* into the sandy bed of the river, and the builders prevent further sinking by stringing a

network of raffia and liana ropes around the foundation
poles, as near as possible to the river bed. This holds up
the main structure on something of a snowshoe principle.
In the space beneath these flimsy abodes are moored the
dugout canoes, locally called pirogues, in which the men-
folk set out to fish after the sun is down. From water
level a rope ladder runs up to a platform which extends
forward of the roofed part of the dwellings and, as we
passed by, naked pickaninnies came out on these porches
to wave and sing. Before dawn the catches of these night
fishermen are in the native retail markets at Leopoldville
and Brazzaville, or have been sold to African fish merchants for the preparation of the smoked fish which plays
such a disproportionately large part in the native's diet.

The approach to Bamu is difficult; the reeds grow out
a hundred yards or more into the water. There were few
channels wide enough to take our boat, for the native
canoes are so much narrower, and there was also the
danger of fouling the screw in the tough, dense *matiti*.
At length we found a place where the bank had been
cut away and the undergrowth cleared, and here we were
greeted by the entire population of the near-by village,
led by a lad of about fifteen who turned out to be the
son of the headman and by trade a maker and mender of
fishing nets. In the welcoming group were also included
three or four inquisitive goats.

We stepped ashore onto a square which was surrounded on three sides by neat little huts, one of which—
the headman's—was larger than the others and had a
strikingly modern annex in the form of a timber shed

with tongued-and-grooved boards and a padlocked door. As I looked round I began to envy that old headman: he had a house, a pigeon roost and about twenty goats. He could never lack for pigeon pie, goat's meat (which is delicious, rather like mutton but less greasy), milk or cheese. He had chickens galore and an abundance of fruit trees.

When we first arrived the native boy had greeted us in French, but we soon found that *"Bon jour, messieurs"* was the only French he knew. However, we got by easily enough on Henri's fluent Lingala. Invited by the headman, we squatted on woven raffia mats with the men of the village; the women remained giggling in their huts. Then the secret behind the padlock was revealed. The old man produced a key from his loincloth, walked over to the shed, unlocked it and produced a set of very fine china, obviously his pride and joy. This he set out on what looked suspiciously like a GI blanket and we sat around while he produced hard-boiled eggs, a hand of bananas, a big ripe pineapple and a *chikwangé*, the latter a sour but not unpleasant native bread made from manioc flour which is dampened, wrapped tightly in a banana leaf, bound with grass and left to ferment a little.

We shared our tinned fruit juice and sandwiches with the villagers, and all in all we made a very good meal. As we wandered around afterward we found that the village had a big plantation of *loofahs*, while behind the huts there were manioc, mangoes, sweet corn, bananas and avocado pears. There were no vegetables.

In addition it turned out that the headman was also a

night fisherman and as a side line collected medicinal roots and herbs in the waterside forest, the roots of whose trees are permanently submerged. It was all very much like the story of the Swiss Family Robinson without the lions and tigers; we did not even see a crocodile that day, and the Congo and its tributaries teem with them.

It was late afternoon when we started back, and as we passed the river-dwellers' huts the fishermen were just getting ready for their night's work. Some were already paddling off, five or six of them to a boat. With an uncanny sense of balance they maneuver these keelless craft, standing up and rowing in perfect unison with short, sharp strokes. They were too intent to wave to us, so we chugged past them and back to the rush-hidden inlet where Henri kept his two boats. When I think today of Africa's past, I still see the island of Bamu; yet even there the changing present was with us in the form of a dinner service of expensive modern Limoges china.

Those who would catch a glimpse of the villages of the old Africa and see something of native everyday life as it has been for centuries—and as it will continue for years despite all the Ten-Year Plans—can take to a river and road trail which leads from Leopoldville to Stanleyville and eastward by a variety of routes to the coast of the Indian Ocean at Mombasa or Dar es Salaam.

Though much is made of the native's rush to the cities and the detribalized zones of the commercial and industrial areas, eighty-five per cent of Central Africa's people still hold to the peasant life. The villages lie strung out along the banks of the great river and its countless tributaries—there is always a stream near a native settlement in the Lower Congo—or in sheltered spots near a water hole in the savanna lands where the herdsmen roam. The village architecture, which is a quick, tangible yardstick of their progress, varies with their accessibility, the wealth of the inhabitants and the local building medium. Permanent dwellings are becoming much more common, and a house in *matière durable* is the ambition of every progressive African, though mud and wattle, impermanent but serving the purpose, are still the commonest building materials in all the villages outside the limits of the cities.

In the areas still only lightly touched by the hand of progress, the three most usual types of dwelling are the rectangular with a sloping roof, the cylindrical with a conical roof, or the round, beehive huts, more frequently found among the shepherds, both Nilotic and Bantu of Ruanda-Urundi and the eastern highlands. These three types are very standardized, and there are few, if any, subdivisions and a complete lack of architectural variety. The artist in the Bantu comes out quite often in his mural decorations. These are usually on the outside walls of the huts and range from intricate geometrical designs (especially in areas where Moslem culture has left a mark) to pictures and story drawings based on such things as hunting adventures, fishing tales with the usual exaggerations, or a journey in a train.

Inside the huts there are beds made of wattles and covered with grass-fiber quilts, woven mats, bench seats or stools and a variety of pots, both iron and earthenware.

Since, except at night, Africans spend their lives in the open air, the insides of their dwellings are more often than not drab and bare. I suppose the natural beauties of Africa's outdoors provide what color and charm they need in their lives.

From the South Atlantic coast to Leopoldville, the Congo rapids close the river to navigation, and to ensure the development of the Congo's interior from the west as well as from the east the Matadi-Leopoldville railway—the first great engineering achievement in this part of Africa—was built. I was in Leopoldville for the fiftieth-anniversary celebrations of the winning of this *Bataille du Rail* (Battle of the Railroad). Fighting for years against tropical diseases, labor troubles, landslides and floods, the pioneers pushed the iron road from the great river port to the sleeping village of Kinshasa. Now, from the metropolis at the head of the rapids, the air lanes fan out and the "wet-tailed Janes" plow their way upstream into the deep green jungle which lies over many, many horizons.

The lower basin of the Congo is practically windless—the international airport at Leopoldville has only one landing strip. Except when the tornadoes are on their way the air is still and more often than not sodden with moisture. But out on the river there is always a breeze, and stepping on board in the early morning haze, leaving behind the still, perspiring humidity of the city, is one of the most gratifying sensations I have ever known. Some of the charm of river travel has been lost now that the diesel boats churn ceaselessly on by day and night, but

there are still some of the older wood-burning boats ply-
ing their way up and downstream and it is to these you
must turn for the fullest enjoyment of a voyage into this
maze of rivers with their shallows, swamps, fast currents
and lazy swells. The banks are always green—there are
few deciduous trees in the Congo—and as the boat
swishes along the eye is mesmerized by the unnatural
brilliance of the foliage and the paler greens, blues and
grays of a background in constant metamorphosis. In the
clearings are native villages with blue smoke rising lazily
from the countless fires; silent men and giggling girls
stand on the banks, watching, and all too often dreaming
of the city with its cycles, zoot suits, phonographs and
movies. *Maybe soon. It can't be long now; Dominique
must come and fetch me one day soon.*

At sunset the wood-burners tie up at little landing
stages to take on fuel supplies. The night is spent aboard
and the next leg of the journey begins as the faintest tinge
of gray appears on the ripples. These landing stages have
become small trading posts, and the native ivory and
basketware sellers show themselves sharp hands at a bar-
gain. Songs are sung, lies—but fascinating lies—are told
in broken French over the aromatic fires; out on the
rough quay the voyager's eyes dance to the rhythm of
the jostling dugout canoes tied alongside and his nose
wrinkles at the smell of fish and the acrid sweat of the
villagers.

These trips never failed to induce in me a feeling of
rebellion against the planners and all their works. Are
the sociologists, economists, industrialists in London,

Paris, Brussels and Lisbon doing what they are because their humanitarian ideals demand that the natives have the same living conditions, the same tastes, the same senses of guilt and shame as they? Or do we have to inflict our ways of life on these grand, simple people because our industrial revolutions and social and economic philosophies, mingled with our national prides and prejudices, have precipitated us into a struggle for existence? Are we dragging them down to our level? The next morning I would always see the other side of the canvas; but to experience mental conflict, I had only to spend a night in a riverside settlement.

There is a gentle sadness, too. One of these nights I met Antoine. He was about fifteen, a sturdy lad with a rich smile and what I mistook at first to be a "slow take." He had in his hands a book which turned out to be a copy of the Bible translated into Lingala, the *lingua franca* of the riverain peoples of the Lower Congo. This book, a well-printed, sturdy job with the conventional black cover and red page edgings, was sold by one of the Protestant missions at a cost, so Antoine told me, of twenty-five francs—fifty cents. From the maze of strange words I could pick out *Abalami*, and since we were looking at the Book of Genesis, it was reasonable to suppose that *Abalami* was the patriarch Abraham. I know a little more about these Bantu languages now. They are comparatively simple, but that does not mean that they are deficient in any way as is so often alleged. On the contrary they are rich in metaphor. "It hurts a little," for example, becomes, "It is eating me with small teeth."

There are just as many subtleties in Bantu dialects as there are in the more complex tongues. But it is fairly easy to learn a kitchen variety of any of the Bantu languages, and in learning, the reason for the mystifying spelling of the patriarch's name is to be seen. There is no rolled "r" sound in these tongues—"r" becomes "l." The African can very rarely put two consonants together, so the "br" in Abraham has to become "bar." And since our friends cannot pronounce "r" anyway, the middle of the word changes to "bal." Hence *Abalam-i*. "P" also defeats the native tongue; pronounced in English, "last supper" would be "las-a-t subber." I was always "Msa Cookiso the Inkileyz." But whether or not you understand them, the Bantu tongues, when well spoken, make pleasant listening and have very soft, agreeable inflections. That same night Antoine showed me a simple book on first aid, printed in French. "I'm learning *premier soins*," he said. I wanted to know why. "It will be useful when I go to the city." My heart sank. Sure enough, he left his father's little farm and fishing business and turned up one day in the city. He wanted a job and I found him one as a messenger boy. A week later he moved on to something else. I never saw him again.

In the riverside settlements, too, are to be found some of the last of the pioneers: traders, plantation overseers, guides, sometimes a little of all three. As in the early days they are of all nationalities, though Belgians, Greeks and Portuguese predominate. The halfway house between Leopoldville and Stanleyville is Coquilhatville, "Coq" to the whites and Wangata to the natives. Why must the

Belgians always change pretty-sounding African names for clumsy European ones? Coquilhatville, named after its first *chef de poste* Coquilhat, lies astride the equator and has the unenviable reputation of possessing the Congo's most trying climate, which must put it well in the running for being the worst in the world. Yet, set though it is in the heart of the equatorial rain-forest area, Coquilhatville has attracted over 600 whites as permanent residents. For transients there are two hotels; there are also a bank, a pharmacy, an airport and a fair shopping district. An energetic body of Catholic priests and nuns, the Protestant Disciples of Christ and the witch doctors, the latter often working underground, struggle for the allegiance of the city's 10,000 Africans. A drab, unadorned place, Coquilhatville's only color lies in the background of some of its inhabitants. The steaming jungles can attract the hardy souls just as strongly as the Arctic wastes. Such a soul was Eugenio Muñoz.

For the past three years I have had only my dreams to bring back the face of Eugenio Muñoz. It was a face of which I became very fond: a sallow, Spanish face with an incongruously red nose and lips curved even in sleep into a smile which laughed with you and at you. The eyes in the face flashed, the even teeth glistened, the graying black hair shone under dime-store pomade. Across the upper lip, slick as a pencil stroke, was the mustache of a swashbuckling pirate. Even without such adornments as golden earrings and a black eyepatch it was the face of a buccaneer.

The body that went with the face was disappointing. It was short and rotund, the arms swung lazily and the noble head itself was set to one side and slightly forward of a pair of plow-horse shoulders. There were carbuncle scars on the neck.

But the voice was soft and pleasant. Spanish rolled from the smiling lips as it must have rolled from the tongues of Philip's grandees; the colorful oaths could be a chaste melody to ears which had no understanding of Spanish blasphemy. Wherever you may be now, Eugenio, you're getting by, for the Lord has a special providence for the wayfarer who drifts along on a sunbeam. Gunrunning in Tangier? Sugar planting in the Seychelles? A sherry waiter at the Casa Martinez in London? Selling lottery tickets in Cuba? No matter where you are, *te saluto*.

Eugenio Muñoz claimed to have Spanish gypsy blood. He certainly played the Romany on a grand scale. It was Muñoz who proved to me that the golden days of adventure are not over in spite of ships and planes and trains which run to dreary schedules set down confusingly in dusty little timetables, the modern travelers' Bibles. Muñoz went where he willed and when he willed, and no physical barrier, not even the Pacific, could hold him back.

On August 17, 1947, this tubby little Spaniard decided to honor the city of Leopoldville with his presence. Two months later I met the newcomer for the first time. Though something of a fish out of water, he was nonetheless doing a creditable job as Spanish-language editor and news writer for the South American programs of the

Belgian Broadcasting Service. The newsroom was a babel of European and African tongues. Muñoz quickly dubbed it "*La cage aux perroquets,*" a name which stuck long after he was gone. I used to share a studio with him when I was broadcasting to America in English, and through many months we sat facing each other during the night watches, smoking, drinking coffee and coaxing that most exacting of mistresses, the microphone.

As he talked with suave tongue and florid gesture I learned many things about this extraordinary man. A veteran of the Chaco war between Bolivia and Paraguay, Muñoz had been a colonel in the Paraguayan Army. South America at peace bored him, so he headed back to the Mediterranean, did a little smuggling around the Dodecanese Islands, then shipped aboard a Greek freighter bound for Newfoundland. He liked the look of the city of Saint John's and, with his customary disregard for visas and other international travel regulations, he jumped ship, only to be incarcerated in one of His Majesty's prisons until a boat could be found to take him away. This ejection from Newfoundland did not embitter him against the British Commonwealth. He was just *settling down*—a statement I found unbelievable—as a ranch hand on an Australian sheep farm when the outbreak of the Spanish Civil War brought him hastening to his native Málaga. He had no strong feelings about either side, managed to pick the loser and as a result is most unlikely to go back to Spain as long as dictator Franco is in power. He was quite philosophical about the fact that he could just as easily have picked the winning side and possibly finished his already eventful career as a military governor in Río de Oro or some such place within the Spanish dominions.

As the Estimado Señor Eugenio Muñoz, he lived for some time in Casablanca, doing, as he put it, "the best I could," a term which usually covers currency peddling or black marketeering. Then, after spending what he referred to as his "intellectual episode" in Leopoldville, he moved upcountry. For a time he had an interest in a trucking business in Coquilhatville, but when I last inquired about him he had gone, leaving nothing but a smile.

Muñoz' kind are scattered all along the Congo's life lines. Many of them must be numbered among the exploiters. They are not interested in the country's political evolution except insofar as new legislation might affect their profits and the status of their workers. However, those of them who do not choose to return to their homelands to spend the money they have made will, with the inborn adaptability of their kind, be able to fit into whatever new social pattern may emerge.

Stanleyville—Singitini in Lingala or Kisangani in Kiswahili—is one of the oldest settlements in the Congo basin, and today one of the fastest growing. Approaching from Ponthierville some seventy miles to the south and still thinking he was making his way down the Nile, Stanley, in January 1877, sighted the falls above where the city now stands. Henry Morton Stanley, journalist turned explorer, was then halfway through his checkered career. He was a flamboyant, enthusiastic and not too likable character, whose native Welsh aggressiveness was heightened by the ups and downs of his early childhood and youth. Stanley was an adopted name, his real name being John Rowlands, a Welsh name if ever there was one. He took the name Henry Morton Stanley out of gratitude to a New Orleans merchant who had befriended him when he arrived in America following his escape from an Oliver Twist existence in a mid-nineteenth-century workhouse.

Stanley served for a short time with the Confederate Army, but his capture at Shiloh brought his military career to an abrupt close, and we next hear of him as a war correspondent. He was sent with a punitive expedition against marauding Indians; he was present when the British invaded Abyssinia in 1868. But it was not until 1871 that he achieved real prominence, for in this year he was sent by John Gordon Bennett, Jr., of the New York *Herald* to find David Livingstone, the missionary-explorer, who was rumored lost. Stanley was for a time an American citizen: he took United States citizenship in 1862, but in 1895 resumed his British nationality, was knighted and sat in the House of Commons in London. Stanley once tried to interest Britain in the Congo. With typical enthusiasm he wrote: "I could demonstrate to you [the British public] that the powerful Congo River, in spite of its cataracts, could absorb the entire traffic of the enormous hinterland. This river is, and will be, the great

waterway for all trade with the center of West Africa."
Nothing came of this overture to British interests, and
Belgium—or rather King Leopold II—stepped in.

Around Stanleyville there occurred the series of clashes
which determined to a large extent the pattern of the
culture which was to be superimposed on that of the
Bantu peoples of the Upper Congo. Arab penetration
into the area of the great lakes of Africa and even farther
westward had been spreading terror among the Negro
inhabitants, since each successive Arab incursion meant
more slave raids with all the attendant misery of shipment down the Nile Valley or from Dar es Salaam and
the east coast ports to the centers of the Islamic world
where further degradations awaited.

White penetration of the area of Kisangani began in
the period between 1850 and 1880, a time of intense
exploration which gave new impetus to the race for
colonies and kindled national rivalries, some of which
have hardly burned themselves out today. Burton and
Speke discovered Lake Tanganyika; Samuel Baker saw
Lake Albert and believed he had discovered the source
of the Nile. The Austrian explorer Schweinfurth penetrated to the land of the Pygmies. Then came Livingstone, believing that Lake Tanganyika gave birth to the
Nile.

The first whites in the Stanleyville area were of several nationalities. Few in number and uncertain of the
temper of the surrounding tribes—some of which were
Arabized and fanatically Moslem—they tried to nego-
tiate with influential local Arabs and met with trouble

right from the start. The most powerful Moslem leader of that decade, Bwana Simba Mabruka (The Glorious Lion), had settled near Stanleyville in 1882, and relations between the Europeans and the Arabs deteriorated slowly until 1886 when a series of minor clashes led to a shooting war. In spite of a treaty made between the explorers and a prominent slave dealer, Tippo Tip, under the terms of which the Arabs had undertaken not to push beyond the Kisangani cataracts in search of slaves, a band of marauders 500 strong presented itself near the Kisangani post during the month of April 1886 with an ultimatum demanding the withdrawal of all Europeans from the area. A Scotsman named Deane, to whom Stanley had confided the command of the post, refused to deal with the Arabs, and shots were exchanged. With the Belgian Lieutenant Dubois and a handful of Hausa soldiers from West Africa, Deane held on for three days, but when the men began to lose heart they decided to burn the post and move down river. In this operation Dubois was drowned and Deane was forced to take refuge with a friendly Bantu tribe, the Bakumu, where he was later discovered by Coquilhat.

Stanley, who was at that time on his way to Zanzibar, proposed that Tippo Tip should enter the service of the Congo Free State and conferred on the Arab leader the title *Vali* (governor) of the Falls. Stanley hoped by this maneuver to put an end to Arab attacks on Europeans in the neighborhood and to limit the activities of the slave raiders, but there was a flare-up some five years later when the remnants of a European exploring party arrived

at Kisangani to tell the gruesome story of the massacre of
their comrades by an Arab band.

Tippo Tip was away in Zanzibar when the stragglers
arrived, but his nephew, Rashid, who, if we believe only
half the atrocity stories told about him, was something of
a monster, assumed charge of the operations, counter-
attacked the enraged whites and drove them with their
African levies back to the right bank of the river. There
was more trouble in May 1893, when Rashid embarked
on a campaign against those Bantu tribes which had
shown any disposition to be friendly toward the Europeans, set fire to their villages and massacred the inhabitants. He then turned once more on the whites at Kisangani, but reinforcements which arrived while the
beleaguered garrison was still putting up a stiff fight
drove the Arabs off and pursued them to Kirundu, where
they gave Rashid's men a sound drubbing and took 1,500
prisoners. There was no further trouble, and in 1898 the
present city of Stanleyville began to take shape on the
right bank of the Congo River.

I think few of us realize how close the Arabs came to
dominating this part of Central Africa. Before the opening of the Suez Canal, all traffic to India and the Indies,
the Far East, Australia and New Zealand had to go
around the Cape of Good Hope. The new waterway,
which came under British domination when Disraeli
negotiated the purchase of the shares of the bankrupt
Egyptian Khedive Ismail in 1875, opened up a quicker
route to India and turned the serious attention of the
European powers to the east coast of Africa for the first

time since the days of the early Portuguese voyagers. At Dar es Salaam, Zanzibar and Mombasa the newcomers found strongly Arabized populations governed by the descendants of the Arab traders who had been developing the trading routes between the Near East and the East African coast and interior since as early as the thirteenth century.

Arab influence quickly becomes much less obvious as we go south from Khartoum on the branches of the Nile, vanishes almost entirely in the Christianized uplands of Ethiopia, but becomes more evident again along the coastal fringe from Kismayu, on the equator, to Dar es Salaam. These Arabs of the coast, linking forces with the few who had made their way down the White Nile and across the Great Lakes region, established a regular route to Zanzibar and began a deep and systematic penetration into the Congo basin in search of slaves for the opulent princes and merchants of the Ottoman Empire. This Arab tide was continuing to mount when the Europeans came, and a struggle was inevitable from the first. Had the white explorers come even ten years later they could not have established themselves without meeting much more serious opposition than they actually did. Nowadays the fast-developing region around Stanleyville reflects its prosperity in schools, hospitals, factories, hotels, a busy river port, a lively air crossroads and a population of 50,000.

5

Bantu Religion

THE MISCELLANY of types and creeds to be seen around Stanleyville made me aware that the religious factor should not be discounted when speculating on how this tangled skein of Africa's future may be unraveled. In this region it is not unusual to see brightly turbaned Moslems with elaborate mother-of-pearl inlaid walking sticks mingling with priests in panamas and white cassocks, nuns with ridiculously oversized sun helmets atop their veils, and—not the least conspicuous—Protestant missionary ladies in their uniform of "sensible" flat-heeled shoes, mass-produced one-piece print dresses and wide-brimmed straw hats set square above their unpowdered faces.

Stanleyville is the geographical center of Africa and a good point at which to see something of the forces, other than political and economic, which are burrowing into the continent's heart. The *new* religions—by which are meant Catholic and Protestant Christianity and Mo-

hammedanism—are struggling to overthrow the triad of
Bantu religion, occultism and sheer animism. The missionaries are making a great deal of headway on paper.
There is no doubt that fair progress is being made, but
the proportion of enthusiastic converts is small; by far
the larger number of Africans who embrace the new
religions are nominal Christians whose conversion has
been wrought by what they imagined was personal expediency, or by their inability to stand aloof from mass
conversions in which entire villages are sometimes involved. The mantle of Christianity sits lightly on these
folk, and backsliding is frequent.

The Moslems have made more headway in Uganda,
Kenya and Tanganyika than they have in the Belgian
Congo. In South Africa, where they are in the main
Indian immigrants, their numbers increase commensu-
rately with that racial element, while in French Equatorial Africa such Moslems as there are hail originally
from West Africa or from the Sahara fringe. The fact
that Islam is steadily strengthening its grip seems to belie
the claim that its devotees no longer proselytize in Central
Africa, and I could have produced additional evidence
a year or so ago in the form of a booklet—which I have
since mislaid—which told in English and French of the
evangelistic mission of Islam and the benefits of being a
disciple of the Prophet. This pamphlet was pressed on
me at Leopoldville one morning by a rich Nigerian trader
named McDonald who was just about to take off by air
on a pilgrimage to Mecca.

Most of Central Africa's cities now have Moslem

mosques, or at least meeting places. Some of them are
crude; others, like the mosque at Poto-Poto—Brazzaville's
native city—have delicate minarets, Arab doorways and
latticework and look as though they had been transported on magic carpets from Cairo or Bagdad. These
mosques are well maintained, and their locations in the
teeming native quarters stimulate the curiosity of the
more intelligent Africans, particularly the merchant
classes. Yes, Islam is just as direct in its approach as are
the various Christian groups, and its success is doubtless
due to the fact that while it insists on an uncompromising
monotheism—a tenet not difficult for the Bantu to absorb—it makes no attacks on polygamy and the discard-
ing of unwanted wives and does not emphasize its
educating mission.

The Roman Catholics and the Anglicans, the most
realistic and efficient of the Christian missionary bodies,
will admit when pressed that their statistics concerning
native Christians are just so many figures, and for that
reason they are often reluctant to publish them. On the
brighter side it can be said that there is a growing number of firm, believing Christians among the Africans.
Not a few Africans have already become priests or ministers and these sturdy, pious folk, with their knowledge
of Christian doctrine and their ability to apply it, will
form a bulwark against the eventual onslaughts of athe-
istic communism—not that the Communists at this stage
would be likely to make a frontal attack on the African's
religion be it Christian, Moslem or Bantu.

The religion of the Bantu peoples has much in com-

mon with the cults of other primitive races, and in the
Bantu conception of the universe are to be found striking
similarities to Biblical lore. In the Bantu cults there are
the threefold elements, much as there are in Christianity,
namely the manes, or souls of the dead, the nonhuman
spirits and a deity. The existence of a soul which is translated to a spirit world at death is a cornerstone of the Central African creeds. The Bantu, however, believes that the
spirit world exists within the boundaries of the physical
world—which includes the firmament—and these disem-
bodied essences, for which an unchanged though invisible
nature is assumed, are held to remain in sympathy with
the living, experiencing the same needs and desires. From
these articles of faith it is a short step to the justification
of acts of human sacrifice and voluntary immolation: if
the spirit of a man continues to need a full family life,
then, according to the Bantu, it is logical that his wife or
maybe wives or female slaves should be sacrificed as part
of the funeral rite. The practice of immolation has died
out, but belief in the material needs of the spirit persists;
and it is not unusual to find in villages up and down the
country small altars erected at the entrance gates or in
the graveyards and bowls of rice, manioc, bread and
other food put out to furnish the spiritual tables. In return for these favors the spirits are said to keep watch
over the living, by whom they can be consulted on
everyday matters and in behalf of whom they can inter-
cede with the superior powers.

The spirit world is, so the Africans say, populated with
the souls of all types of living creatures, but there is no

transmigration. The souls of humans are reincarnated only in humans. Those of dogs return to dogs and those of crocodiles to crocodiles. This firm belief that animals have souls has led to an integration of animal spirits with the general conception of the universe, but it is not true to claim, as some early writers have, that certain creatures, crocodiles in particular, are credited by the Bantu with supernatural powers and sometimes even worshiped. It *is* true that the Bantu and the crocodile eye each other with respect; their physical encounters are more often than not the result of human provocation and have proved fatal to one or both parties too frequently for them to be treated lightly. What does happen sometimes is that a tribe, or even a number of tribes, have an emblem, and this distinguishing sign, whether it be animal, vegetable or mineral, is revered or even eventually held sacred. In the course of time taboos are attached to it: that is to say, it must not be touched or harmed by any desecrating hand.

The existence of an all-powerful deity is generally assumed by the Bantu; yet in their creed there is no provision for any worship of this supreme creator and disposer of the world. Africans often go to the opposite extreme, even to the point of not mentioning the name of the All-Powerful, so as not to draw attention to themselves.

The third element, spirits of nonhuman origin, provides what complications exist in African Negro religious philosophy. Like angels and devils these spirits are good and bad, and anything which cannot be explained in terms of reality or the other two religious elements is attributed to the nonmaterial spirits which, like Gabriel and Lucifer, have existed since the creation. The work of the good spirits is to be seen in gentle rain and sunshine, the ripening of the crops and material prosperity. Their benevolence is unobtrusive and they are spoken of with quiet reverence.

But thunder, lightning and earthquake are other manifestations which could not be described by primitive men in physical terms, and such phenomena were quite naturally considered the work of spirits less well-disposed toward mankind. Here lies the province of the African soothsayer: flood, pestilence and famine are the handiwork of unfavorable occult powers, and to ward off these evils the anger of the spirits has to be assuaged. Apart from asking the intercession of ancestral spirits, which is simple prayer, a vast system of fetishism has evolved down the years, and amulets, talismans and magic recipes are sold by the witch doctors, who, to do them justice, are more often than not conscientious practitioners of "white magic."

Yet it cannot be said that the Bantu religion is fetishistic; the untutored may attribute magic powers to the fetishes themselves, but I have had it made clear to me by both white and native sages that the powers of these objects, which are often no more than a carved clothespin or a piece of rag, lies in the charm or incantation which has been offered over them. Here is a striking parallel with the practices of cults with inflexible doctrines, complicated liturgies and codes of very positive moral laws. I am sure that to a large extent the greater success of the Catholic and high-Anglican churches in the mission field may be attributed to the fact that the elements of Christianity can be instilled through Catholic teaching without occasioning the wholesale destruction of the native's beliefs. I have found large numbers of tribesmen embracing Protestantism as an ethic, but keeping fetish rags wrapped round their fingers, just in case. The Catholic dogma of the communion of saints and their powers of intercession, supported by such tangibles as crucifixes, statues and rosaries blessed by the Pope, finds ready response in the African and leads to an easier assimilation of the other fundamentals. In many cases, though, as I have pointed out, primitive beliefs are slow a-dying, and what the first generation of Christianized blacks really understands of its new religion is a matter for doubtful speculation.

The similarity of Bantu conceptions of the world and the early books of the Old Testament can be seen in the mythology of the Baluba, one of the more advanced tribes of the Kasai and the industrialized Katanga province of the Belgian Congo. Like other Bantu peoples they place the divinity, Nzambi, and the other nonhuman spirits in an inaccessible world and reserve their prayers for the spirits of their ancestors.

According to the Baluba, when the soul leaves the body it follows the Milky Way, which is the road separating the world of good from the world of evil. At the crossroads along the Milky Way, where the paths of earth and heaven cross with those of paradise and hell,

lies the mystic river Ata, and once across this Bantu
Styx the soul comes to judgment. On the far bank of the
Ata the sky-borne soul is awaited by a jury of four good
and four evil spirits, and if it is found to be pure, it is
conducted along the eastern branch of the heavenly road
toward the Village of Sweet and Floury Bananas. If on
the other hand the soul is found to be wanting, it takes
the western road to the infernal gulf, the bottomless pit
of red earth.

In the tranquil Village of Bananas every created thing,
be it an animal, a plant, or a human soul at rest, is of the
purest white. Peace and joy are absolute. This is the
center of the domain of Mulemuedi and his four good
angels, a land of smooth paths and many crossroads, at
each of which is a celestial village where the souls of the
blest live as they lived on earth. Feasting, loving, rejoicing, they await the day of their reincarnation.

Before their return to the world of humans these pure
spirits move to a limbo in the Milky Way where they
become shooting stars, finally extinguishing themselves
and falling down to earth to enter the body of a newborn
infant.

The western path—the road to hell—curves back to an
earthly inferno where the spirits of the damned lie in
hunger, thirst and every physical torment, their eyes
slowly blinded by the glare which comes from the bottomless pit of red earth. These unfortunates have no
hope of reincarnation: they are forever subject to Kavi-
dividi, the fallen angel, and his four demon lackeys.

Before his rebellion against the good spirits Kavi-dividi was an angel of good will, but in his fall he tried, and almost succeeded, in bringing the whole human and animal world down with him to the red gulf. But good triumphed and only the dupes of the devil went with him: the good remained in paradise where they still undergo successive reincarnations which will continue until the end of time. This view of heaven and hell, with the angels of purity and joy, and Kavi-dividi and his demons could be a rewrite of the early Hebrew beliefs.

Bantu religions have no set prayers, no special forms of service for significant occasions and no corporate worship. The one rite to which great importance is attached and which has more or less the same character across the continent from the Atlantic to the Indian Ocean is that of circumcision. Circumcision of both sexes is common, and its importance lies in that it signifies the transition from the adolescent to the adult stage. The whole practice is shrouded with contrived mystery, and the ceremonies, timed to coincide with certain phases of the moon, are attended with weird noises and trick manifestations in order to impress on the minds of the initiates the importance of the ritual in which they are partaking.

Prior to the physical act of circumcision there are orgies of feasting, drinking and dancing, following which the youngsters disappear into the forest or some other secluded place with the circumcisers. They remain away from their villages until they are completely healed, usually a matter of ten days, and on their return the newly circumcised are faced with a series of tests designed to prove that they are worthy of their new adult

status. Finally they are instructed in the significance of
the mysteries which are withheld from the uncircum-
cised. Though ritual circumcision is still widely practiced
among the forest tribes, it is becoming of lesser importance in the lives of the tribes which have been brought
into contact with some of the aspects of the twentieth
century. Nevertheless a pretense of retaining the old
custom is still made, though the initiates are usually as
familiar with the stage setting, the weird noises and the
claptrap as American teenagers are familiar with the
legend of Santa Claus.

Striking east from Stanleyville on what is, for the
Congo, a good road, the traveler finds that the atmosphere
becomes clearer and cooler. By the time Irumu is reached
the air has a highland freshness, while at Bunia, nearer
the shore of Lake Albert, the climate has become almost
temperate and the vegetation has a European look. This
eastbound road leads up to the land of the Pygmies, the
Batwa as they are called. Beyond Nia-Nia on the road
from Stanleyville to Lake Albert lies the Ituri forest, the
reservation, so to speak, of the Pygmies. Here they dwell
amid giant trees which tower 150 feet above the ground,
with dog-faced baboons and the rare okapi—found only
in the Belgian Congo—as neighbors; unseen, they observe
every movement of the passer-by.

The ways of the Pygmies are known to very few white
men, though in some places more is being learned about
them as they begin to lose their shyness. Realizing that
the European has no hostile intentions, they come bash-

fully forward and will even, if suitably rewarded—the "tip" has become universal—allow themselves to be photographed. The fact that the Pygmy is beginning to overcome his reticence can be ascribed to the life and character of such men as Patrick Putnam, an American who lives close to the Pygmies' haunts and who knows more about them, and about the flora and fauna of the region in general, than any other man alive. Putnam, a lean, bearded scientist, no lover of cities, has a rest camp at Epulu, about three hundred miles northeast of Stanleyville. When I was in Leopoldville he used to come down now and again, and when he did he went quietly about his business of buying supplies or shipping off zoological specimens, driving around in a battered old blue car which, being the same hue as the equatorial sky, was the only thing that led us to notice his presence. Sipping the excellent Leopoldville beer, he would play a few games of chess, and then just as quietly as he arrived he would slip back into his green wilderness—back to his Pygmies.

Homer, Aristotle and Herodotus mention the Pygmies: they use the Greek word *pugmaios*—one cubit tall—and relate many picturesque legends concerning their origin. The ancient Egyptians knew them, and they have been depicted on Egyptian monuments. On one such monument there is a fair representation of a Pygmy above the name *Akka*, a name still borne by a Pygmy tribe which inhabits the Uele region in the northern Congo.

The origin of these little people is unknown. It is certain that they were in Africa before the Bantu migrations and that their culture was, and still is, with the possible exception of that of the South African Bushman, the most primitive among all African races. It is not even certain how long they have been forest dwellers, but today the true Pygmies, hunters to a man, set themselves apart from both Bantu and white man, roving the forests in search of game. They are cunning to a degree, hunting with bows, arrows and crude hunting nets, often using poisoned arrows with harpoon-shaped tips which enlarge the wound when pulled out. As a rule Pygmies are not tattooed, and their clothing consists of a loincloth made of beaten bark held up by a length of liana or, in some cases, a rope of bark.

Yet even the Pygmies have been unable to keep their strain pure, and it can truly be said that nowadays there are more pygmoids than there are Pygmies. The pygmoid races of the Congo, Tanganyika and Ruanda-Urundi have varying proportions of Bantu and Sudanese blood and are taller than the Pygmies, averaging five feet two inches for men and four feet ten for women. These people are no longer nomads; they have for the most part settled near, or even in, Bantu villages, and this is merely serving to accelerate their assimilation. The pygmoid groups have begun to cultivate land and are adopting the monetary system of the country in which they live.

The true Pygmy male is rarely more than four feet four inches tall, the female four feet two, while some groups (so I was told; I was never able to substantiate this) average as little as four feet three for the men and four feet one for the women. One hundred pounds is an average weight and the skin of a true pygmy, in contrast

to that of the very black pygmoids, is a yellowish brown.
Now that they are losing their shyness the *Bambuti*—a
term of endearment—have developed a system of barter
with the Bantu chieftains in whose territory they live, by
which they supply meat and surrender the ivory from
the elephants they kill in return for farm products, which
they are using more and more. Generally, Pygmies are
able to speak the language of the tribe or people with
whom they are in closest contact. Alone in the forest
they are said to employ a patois of their own.

The attitude of the Bantu toward the Pygmy can be
defined as a mixture of fear and a rather contemptuous
paternalism: the black tribesman has not forgotten the
day when these little folk were fierce and cruel. But
today there is an easy tolerance on both sides, and no effort is being made to force the *Bambuti* out of their dark
forest retreats. The Pygmies subscribe to no religious
doctrines. In so far as they can be said to have a religion
at all, they are animists, ascribing conscious life to all
natural objects. The Pygmy believes that animals, plants
and even stones are inhabited by souls. So far the missions have made only very slight, if any, penetration of
the Pygmy mind, and in view of the neolithic character
of their culture and their lack of numbers, they are unlikely to play any telling role in future developments in
Africa.

So far, then, it does not appear as though religious issues in Africa are cutting across political lines. Yet this
has happened and is still happening to a wide degree. For
the African is a great joiner of secret societies, of which

there are a great many still in existence. Some of these
organizations can best be described as politico-religious
groups which harness and distort Christian formulas to
serve their particular ends: some pose as mutual-aid societies, while yet others make a direct appeal to the
African's cupidity and bluntly claim to be the means to
personal enrichment. On the extreme fringe of these per-
sonal-enrichment bodies were such villainous bands as the
Aniotos—the Leopard-Men—who for a long time terrorized Africans in the area of the Babali River to the east of
Stanleyville.

Using a mixture of witchcraft and savagery, these men
of the Society of the Leopard struck with their terror
weapon at the full moon. With steel claws attached to
their fingers, they would maim or even kill victims selected quite indiscriminately from the riverain tribes of
the Babali and extract loot from the terrified villagers.
Blinded by blood lust, many Leopard-Men really imagined themselves to be leopards: they roared like leopards,
sprang and killed like them and even drank the blood of
their victims. These unfortunates, if they survived, were
afraid to come forward with complaints, and unharmed
villagers hesitated to lodge information for fear of death
or disfigurement and because of a natural desire to propi-
tiate the leopard spirits which demanded that these outrages be perpetrated.

Leopard-Men were drawn from all classes, from unlet-
tered laborers to clerks and skilled mechanics. At one
time there was no means of knowing whether the clerk
at your grocer's or the taxi man with whom you rode

were Aniotos. Membership in the society called for the most solemn vows of secrecy, and these were enforced by terror. But gradually the authorities pinned down the suspects; and according to the last reports I have, the Society of the Leopard is no more, and its remaining members are in prison in Stanleyville. I'm unable to vouch for this, however, and if events in Kenya are any criterion, another outbreak of leopard terrorism is possible at any time.

The official report of a pre-Mau Mau outburst of terrorism in Kenya sums up admirably the dangers of a little learning and shows how, unless religion is taught with the greatest care to avoid possible misinterpretation, it can be distorted to further the aims of these politico-religious societies. The report says:

Little could they [the missionaries] have guessed that in the space of a few years some of the people they had tried so hard to guide would break away from true Christianity, form their own fanatical sects, and apply their minds to the ugly business of interpreting the Bible to their own ends. . . . To arouse ignorant savages to a frenzy of blood-hate; to incite arson and murder; and to encourage the most virulent form of anti-European African nationalism.

6

Beyond Stanleyville
(Ruwenzori—Kilo Moto—
Elephant Farm)

EAST OF Stanleyville lies the Africa of the tourist. Better roads than those of the Bas-Congo push out toward the mist-clad peaks of the Ruwenzori range. Twenty miles beyond Patrick Putnam's domain at Epulu, near a fork in the road stands a hostelry called the Hotel des Pygmées; why it should be so named I cannot understand, since I doubt that a Pygmy has ever been inside the door. This settlement, which would be dismissed in America as a whistle stop, is Mambasa. Yet Mambasa is a landmark, for it boasts an Emmanuel Protestant Mission and a dispensary, and it is here that the road swings south to Mutwanga at the foot of Ruwenzori, the rallying place of all pilgrims to the shrine of the moon. Words fail, and even pictures cannot begin to convey a true impression of this equatorial paradise. In the second century of our era the Graeco-Egyptian genius Ptolemy wrote: "The Mountains of the Moon, which by their snows feed the lakes, the sources of the Nile." Ptolemy was only partly right, but even 1,800 years ago Ruwenzori was already a mystic legend.

Ruwenzori, the Mountains of the Moon. This mighty range makes live again all the romance of King Solomon's Mines. Who can tell, and who ever will be able to tell, of the love, the strife and the bloodshed which took place on its slopes hundreds, or maybe thousands of years ago. In this region, too, lie the Central African lakes which fill the Albertine Rift, a thirty-mile-wide trench which runs from the upper reaches of the Nile to the Zambezi. Away to the south of Ruwenzori lie the giant volcanoes: Mikeno, Nyamlagira, Nyiragongo, Karisimbi, Visoke, Sabinio, Gahinga and Muhavura. In 1948 Nyiragongo awoke from sleep, sending a slaggy river of lava steaming into the bright-blue waters of Lake Kivu, the highest lake in Africa—a lake which supports almost no life because of the lava pollution and its altitude. There are no crocodiles, no hippopotamuses and very few fish.

Among these African Alps whose summits have the moon as a neighbor is the world of our encyclopedia pictures of the Carboniferous Age forests: ferns thirty feet high, giant lichens and lobelias which dwarf the tallest man—plants of a lost world which live there, and only there.

Ruwenzori was first sighted by a white man about 1840, but Stanley was the first to record the discovery in any detail. In 1888 he was moving to the assistance of the Egyptian governor of the Equatoria province, Emin

Pasha, who was trapped in the south by the Mahdist revolt in the Sudan. Stanley encamped on the Kasenyi
escarpment above Lake Albert in May of that year. From
there he saw the glaciers of the Ruwenzori range which
he took at first, so he relates, to be a peculiarly shaped
cloud.

The Mountains of the Moon are not of volcanic origin,
and their vegetation, ranging from tropical to arctic, re-
tains a strange primeval character which is a constant
source of wonder to the traveler and scientist alike. In
the higher altitudes the lowland palms give way to a
cultivated region abounding in bananas (some of which
are inedible giants eighteen inches long), manioc and
figs. This tropical land of plenty gives way to a sparser
layer of rank grass and monstrous nettles whose needles
can sting through heavy clothing; next come thirty-foot
ferns and giant lobelias which tremble from the assaults
of the sugar hummingbirds that feed on insects caught in
their flowers. More bamboo, orchids, six-foot groundsel,
heather, moss and lichen, then nothing but bare rock,
moving, so it seems, ever upward to the mist-shrouded
land of equatorial snows.

Elephants, buffaloes, gorillas, lions and leopards roam
up to heights of 13,000 feet, seeking the protection of
these defiant mountains. And protection they find. In
1925 when this land was still largely unexplored the
American naturalist Carl Akely led an expedition to
Lake Kivu. On this trip he conceived the idea of a vast
sanctuary, a haven for all hunted creatures, where they
could live their lives unmolested and breed undisturbed.

And so at his instigation the huge national parks of Central Africa began to take shape. The greatest of these, the Albert Park—which embraces Ruwenzori, runs along the border of British Uganda, across Lake Edward, and takes in the volcanoes on its way to the northern shore of Lake Kivu—is an untouchable 2,000,000 acres in which all living things are carefully preserved. No firearms are allowed: the visitor may not even carry a weapon for self-defense and is honor-bound not to introduce any plants or seedlings which are not natives of this strange lost world.

So, quite oblivious of the reason he is not persecuted, the wild beast will roam—free from the grasp of rude hands, the flowers will bloom and even the insects will continue to bite. And away on the horizon the volcanoes and the Mountains of the Moon will nod to each other and say, "This is as we always knew it."

Yet next door to this changelessness is inexorable change. To the north of the mountains and nearing the frontier of the Anglo-Egyptian Sudan we come across one of Africa's many mineral belts, and the heavy hand of industrialization is seen on a landscape which could have held very little attraction to begin with. Perhaps any countryside would look drab and ordinary after the splendors of the Albert Park, but this northern Congo panorama is more than usually gray and dust-laden during the dry seasons. The compensation for this lack of scenic beauty is a heart of gold—large deposits of veinous and alluvial gold. Here are the Kilo-Moto gold mines, a perfect example of the Belgian colonial system at work.

Gold was known to exist in this part of the Ituri region as far back as 1895, but the first gold-bearing gravels were found in the Agola River in 1903 by Hanan and O'Brien, a Cohen-Kelly team of prospectors working for Leopold II's Congo Free State. The African chief in whose territory the discovery was made was named Kilo, and when more profitable deposits were subsequently uncovered in the Moto River the name Kilo-Moto was coined. From the time of the first exploitation until 1919 the gold fields were worked by the Congo Free State and the Belgian government successively, but in the latter year the state authorities handed over control of the enterprise to the *Régie des Mines d'Or de Kilo-Moto*, which in 1925 became the *Société des Mines d'Or de Kilo-Moto*.

The gold deposits are strewn over some 30,000 square miles, and although only alluvions had been worked until coming under private ownership in 1925, over a thousand tons of gold have been produced since the earliest days. In 1951 I was told by a Portuguese mining engineer who knew Kilo-Moto and the Katanga too that the Kilo-Moto mines are now treating 12,000,000 cubic yards of gravel and 800,000 tons of ores a year and are obtaining a total yield of about seven tons of fine gold.

Even with all the machinery available nowadays, more especially since the inception of the Ten-Year Plan, a good-sized labor force is still employed. The story goes that at the beginning of the century when the native was given a wheelbarrow and told to get to work he carried the barrow on his head to the diggings. Now the grandsons of those same natives take an electric shovel as a matter of course.

Over sixty per cent of the company's budget goes in caring for its native labor. According to the *African World*, if one adds to the 25,000 workers—exclusive of the 3,000 or more who are working without a contract— some 20,000 wives and 32,000 children, it can be seen that Kilo-Moto has to look after 80,000 natives.

This labor force is housed in 230 "city" units, having a total of 24,000 laborers' dwellings and 725 better-type houses for African clerks and mechanics. Having thus housed its workers, the company proceeds to look after 80,000 "inner men" by countering the African's traditional improvidence with part-payment in kind. Five hundred tons of foodstuffs grown on company farms, some of which are as much as 100 miles away from the diggings, are conveyed to the native housing estates and distributed each week.

The physical fitness of the force is one of the prime concerns of the administration. Kilo-Moto employs nine doctors, one chemist, seven highly trained medical assistants, seventeen Sisters of Mercy, 462 hospital attendants, nurses and assistants and forty-two certified midwives. It runs eight hospitals, three of which are for European employees, two radiographic stations, a bacteriological laboratory, three maternity homes, three orphanages and 156 dispensaries. And the African workers and their families are treated free of charge.

To educate its natives, Kilo-Moto has set up 136 primary schools with over 150 native teachers and more than 8,000 pupils—the company is planning further improvement here—and runs six "central" (high) schools with 1,500 students. In addition there are professional day schools for miners, hospital assistants and midwives and evening classes at the disposal of the dwellers in most of the "city" units.

Kilo-Moto has built workshops for the upkeep and repair of its machinery; it has forests for its timber supplies, three sawmills and carpenters' workshops. The food supply for the labor is ensured by farms covering 60,000 acres. And as if this were not enough, the directors have sponsored the building and maintenance of a network of roads in the Kilo-Moto area, the port of Kasenye on Lake Albert, regional telephone lines and four hydroelectric power stations generating 12,000 horsepower, an output which is to be practically doubled under the provisions of a new hydroelectric scheme.

This undertaking is by no means unique in the Belgian Congo: the industrial Katanga can provide numerous other instances of similar plans which include even more ambitious health schemes for underground workers, particularly those likely to be affected by silicosis and other occupational diseases. Such workers are supplied with generous quantities of free milk.

Yes, at Kilo-Moto benevolent paternalism is at work and the African proletariat has never had it so good.

And while all this twentieth-century planning is turning the eyes of industrialists and sociologists to Kilo-Moto, the skills of many centuries ago are still being practiced at Gangala na Bodio, which is almost next door by African scales of distance. It often used to be thought that the African elephant could not be trained as a worker. The Gangala na Bodio elephant-training establishment, the only one of its kind in Africa, can offer striking proof to the contrary. In these days of the crane and the bulldozer, the elephant can still hold his own as a worker and, far from disappearing from the labor scene, elephants are being increasingly used in the more inaccessible places.

Leopold II first conceived the idea of domesticating the African elephant, because the great pachyderm is not affected by the bite of the tsetse fly which, until the introduction of vaccines a few years ago, was responsible for the epidemics of sleeping sickness that periodically decimated both human beings and animals. Back in 1879 a convoy of four Indian elephants was landed at Dar es Salaam and brought to the Congo for the purpose of training those captured locally. This experiment was not a success. The Indian elephants pined and all were dead within a year. King Leopold next ordered a certain Commandant (Major) Laplume to undertake the training of young African elephants right from scratch. By 1910 the enterprise was flourishing, and it has never looked back.

Elephants can be trained only if they are caught young. Fifteen years, at which stage they are about six feet high, is the best age according to the hunters and trainers. The hunting party, led by skilled native trackers, locates the elephant herd, maneuvers so that it can be approached from downwind—for the elephant has an uncannily acute sense of smell to compensate for its weak eyesight—then breaks upon the herd at full speed.

Singling out a likely-looking youngster and holding off the adults with rifle fire, the leader of the party lassoes his prey and ties it to a tree. The other elephants are chased off with volleys of shots, an undertaking which often lasts a long time, and trained beasts are brought up from the farm. The captive is pacified, and when he has become more docile he is tied to the leader of the tame band and taken to camp.

Then begins a period of from ten to twelve months' rigorous training—a most delicate task. The newcomer first learns to allow the approach of men, particularly the approach of the native who is to be his driver. Then when he has become more even-tempered he is washed down twice a day, a practice of which he is very fond, and pampered with such delicacies as sweet potatoes, sugar cane, pineapples and bananas. He is a strict vegetarian.

One day the youngster is mounted, at first only for a few moments, then for gradually increasing periods. Next he is taught, mainly by bribery, to obey commands to sit and rise; and the final step in this stage consists of daily walks with a trained elephant which, by some strange sense, is able to forestall any attempts to play rough.

At the end of the training period the elephant has learned how to carry loads and how to haul. Fully trained and fully grown, he is capable of hauling a load of two or three tons on a road or carrying up to 900 pounds on his back. He can also pull two or three-bladed plows. His working day is from five to six hours—not a bad life at all, considering the high standard of board and lodging which goes with it.

7

The Katanga

AT OUR pivotal point, Stanleyville, the Congo—
or the Lualaba as it is known from this point on-
ward—swings to the south, and after by-passing, via
an eighty-mile railroad, the rapids which are scattered
upstream almost as far as Ponthierville, we reach the bank
of the river again at the steamer landing for Kindu, a
three-day voyage away. Kindu, which although remote
I found to be a thriving settlement with 400 Europeans
among 12,000 natives, is the head of yet another of these
Congo road-rail-water transport links: the Kindu-Kon-
golo-Albertville line runs to the shores of Lake Tanganyika, but at Kabalo there is another rail-river change for
the Katanga-bound visitor. At Bukama stand the termi-
nus of the railroad from Port Franqui on the Kasai and
the beginning of the Katanga railroad which runs
through Elizabethville into Northern Rhodesia and right
down to Johannesburg and the Cape.

This southeastern corner of the Congo is the Katanga, at which Cecil Rhodes, the British empire-builder, once looked with envious eyes: in fact he even hinted at its annexation to the British Crown. It is interesting to speculate as to what might have happened if this unparalleled concentration of mineral wealth had been added to Queen Victoria's domains. One thing is certain: the fact that Rhodes's whispers went unheeded has put Belgium in possession of the wherewithal for the successful pursuance of her colonial ambitions.

The scrubby landscape of most of the Southern Katanga, dotted as it is by used-out mine workings and the many-hued hills thrown up by the miners' machines, is depressing, to say the least. Unlike many who profess to see surrealist beauty in a yellowish plain broken up by bald red, yellow and gray mountains, I fail to feel any reaction but mental discomfort pointed up by the physical misery caused by dust-blocked nostrils. The region around Elizabethville has the longest dry season in the entire colony. It lasts about seven months compared with the three or four months in the Kwango and Leopoldville; and at the height of this dusty, uncomfortable stretch, the savanna grass turns brown and the scrubby, dwarfish trees lift their brittle arms in a constant supplication for rain.

Yet the long, rainless periods, the lower humidity and the cool air produce workers more energetic than those found in the steaming heat of Leopoldville, Coquilhatville and the Lower Congo. The natives, too, who were there before the white man came were an energetic and

aggressive crew, quite unlike the languid, peaceable folk
of the humid rain forests. These men of the Katanga
were men of blood and war, and though tribal energies
are now turned along different paths, the old days in the
Katanga linger on in song and story. It is a bare sixty
years since M'Siri died, and with him vanished the most
barbarous native empire Central Africa has ever known,
an organization of terror worse than that of Chaka and
Dingaan, the Zulus who massacred the Boer settlers, and
Lobengula, the Matabele enemy of the British. Yet the
saga began not with gold and diamonds but with copper,
the most widespread of the Katanga's many riches.

The legend, unraveled by René Cornet, a Belgian
writer, tells that some Bayeke hunters from Tanganyika,
while trailing a wounded elephant, came to Nandubesa
in the domain of the great chief Katanga. There they
saw ingots of copper and copper crosses which were used
as money. Some of these they purchased and took back
home to the land of Sumbwa. Kalassa, the chief of the
Bayeke, then came down to visit King Katanga and
formed friendships which lasted many years to the profit
of both peoples. Some years later Kalassa, on another
copper-buying expedition, brought with him his youth-
ful son 'Ngelengwa, later to be hated and feared as
M'Siri; and when the old man Kalassa returned alone to
Tanganyika, he left 'Ngelengwa behind with orders to
maintain friendly relations with the Katanga chieftains.

King Katanga bestowed on M'Siri—as he had become
by then—a well-watered site for a dwelling, little thinking
that here the future tyrant was to gather around him the

barbarous clique through whom he was to control his future empire. M'Siri quickly set to work: he invited to his new home two of his brothers, several of his relatives and a suicide squad of warriors of his Bayeke race. In those earlier days he seems to have been quite without fear, and on the death of Katanga he threw his small force against the sons of his benefactor, defeating them with great slaughter. He exterminated the warriors of Chief Kazembe and put an end once and for all to the foraging raids of the Baluba. His insatiable thirst for battle took him on from victory to victory: the skulls of his enemies adorned his palace walls in ever-increasing numbers. He took from the chiefs he conquered their ivory, salt, iron and copper which he sold to the Arabs on the east coast and the Portuguese trading stations on the western seaboard in return for arms and ammunition for his hordes.

All his district governors and notables had to give him a sister or a daughter not only as a wife (M'Siri is reputed to have had over 700 wives and concubines), but more especially as a hostage to keep his subordinates in line. He even married a beautiful mulatto, Maria de Fonseca, niece of a well-known Portuguese coastal trader, Coimbra. He met Maria when she was traveling in the interior with her uncle, a Portuguese half-breed named Honjo, and took her to his capital city Bunkeya, a stronghold with 20,000 inhabitants and a garrison of 10,000 men, one-third of them armed with guns. He had two cultivated Arab secretaries and even dreamed of marrying a white woman, going so far as to send a messenger to the Portuguese governor of São Paulo de Loanda requesting the hand of one of his daughters.

M'Siri's hatred of whites is said to date from the quite natural refusal of this request. It was for many years thereafter as much as a white man's life was worth to penetrate into M'Siri's kingdom, although in 1886, for some reason which was never explained, he gave a party of British missionaries permission to settle near Bunkeya. Once they were installed, however, he allowed them no freedom of movement, treating them as slaves—a term he used when referring to them.

Old age approached, but the tyrant's empire remained intact. M'Siri had not lost his taste for bloodshed, and when he became too feeble to go forth to war he turned his peculiar talent for cruelty to devising tortures for his wives and courtiers. Women were locked in enclosures with wild creatures to perish and be eaten there; men were buried in a standing position with only their heads showing and left to die, their lidless eyes burned up by the sun. The hearts of his wives were torn out and M'Siri sucked the blood and spat it upon his courtiers as a sign of favor. Men were tied to trees and when they cried out in hunger their ears, noses or arms were torn off and offered to them to eat.

But M'Siri's preoccupation with sadistic tortures allowed his many enemies to organize against him. His empire was beginning to disintegrate: tribute was no longer paid, the mines were deserted. Smoldering resentment at last burst into flame, and the Basanga notables, learning that one of M'Siri's wives, a daughter of their paramount chief, Panda, had been hacked to death during a drinking bout, led a revolt which culminated in the massacre of all the Bayeke living within their territory. The rot had begun to set in, and by the time the Berlin Conference of 1885 defined the Katanga territory as falling within the jurisdiction of the Congo Free State, M'Siri's tyrannous rule was nearing its end.

In order to avoid bloodshed if possible, Captain Stairs, a Canadian in command of the Congo Free State's Katanga expedition, tried at first to parley with M'Siri with a view to pacifying the country and putting an end to the slave trade. M'Siri fled from Bunkeya, and when he defied orders to return, Stairs sent Captain Bodson, a Belgian, to bring the tyrant back to his capital. Threatened by M'Siri, Bodson fired, killing the old monster, but was himself immediately shot and killed by M'Siri's son Masuka. But Bodson, who lies buried in the village of the mulatto queen Maria de Fonseca, had fired the shot which blew the tyrant's empire to pieces. M'Siri's younger son Mukanda Bantu, invested as chief in his father's place, made a complete act of submission to the state, and the blue flag with the gold star, the flag of Leopold II's Congo Empire, rose over yet one more strip of the African wilds.

Bunkeya nowadays bears no traces of its turbulent history. It lies on the left bank of the quiet Bunkeya River, a tributary of the placid Lufira. It has a Catholic mission of the Benedictine fathers and sisters, a Protestant mission, a school, a hospital. A lone, dusty road leads south to the ultramodern industrial town of Jadotville fifty miles away.

The good folk of Elizabethville, Katanga's industrial metropolis, claim that their city is the Congo's second capital, and with good reason. Lubumbashi, as it is still called by the natives, now has a population of over 130,-000, and in spite of the French and Flemish street and shop signs and the adaptations of Flemish architectural styles to be seen in its suburban homes, I always get the feeling that it is here that South Africa begins. It is in fact only a short journey from Elizabethville into Northern Rhodesia, where, at Ndola, we get our first glimpse of the empire created by Cecil Rhodes.

Elizabethville is high as well as dry. It stands at an altitude of 4,000 feet and has spread out over the landscape in forty-five years—in 1909 there was not a house to be seen. The Katanga has developed culturally as well as industrially, and in Elizabethville, Jadotville and the big mining encampments it can fairly be said that the arts have not been neglected. Yet somehow there lacks the soft touch of the Lower Congo: the harsh metallic contents of the soil seem to have been transmitted to the atmosphere, and this is a feeling which persists as we go southward for hundreds of miles, right down into Northern Rhodesia astride Central Africa's gigantic copper belt.

The Belgian Congo, along with Canada and Rhodesia, follows the United States and Chile in the world's copper output, and the Congo alone is producing half as much again as the total output of the Soviet Union, at least according to the figures released by Moscow.

This immense contribution to the world's copper reserves places the Belgian Congo high in the concerns of the United States and the free world, yet in respect of copper—and more particularly in respect of tin production—the cheaper labor used in other countries has provided a source of anxiety to Belgian producers. Tin mining in the Congo began in 1904 when important lodes were discovered at Busanga, Kasongo and Kilole in Katanga province. In 1910 other large deposits were located at Manono near the shores of Lake Tanganyika, and after the First World War immense strikes were made at Maniema and in the Kivu and Ruanda-Urundi. These latter mines are now producing nearly three quarters of the total Congo output of 25,000 tons a year of smelting tin and cassiterite ore. And as yet there is no positive knowledge of the extent of the deposits at Maniema, which were not exploited on a large scale until after 1930.

The Belgian Congo now takes fourth place among the world's tin-producing countries, coming after Indonesia, Malaya and Bolivia. The Western Allies were deprived of the tin from the East Indies and Malaya during the Japanese occupation: with Allied assistance the Belgian authorities stepped up Congolese production from just over 7,000 tons in 1936 to 17,000 tons of metallic tin in 1945. There has been no tailing off since, owing to the continued necessity of meeting increasing demands for civilian and defense production requirements.

Before World War II all the Congo's tin ore was sent to Belgium where the metal was extracted and refined at a plant near Antwerp. When the German occupation of the mother country severed direct relations with the colony refineries were established at Manono and Lubudi, enabling the producers to continue exploiting all the known deposits. Since the war the presence of on-the-spot processing plants has permitted the direct shipment of large quantities of the pure metal to the United States.

Provided prices remain at a remunerative level, there is every chance that the Congo's tin production will continue to rise, especially since the industry is to be helped by the projected hydroelectric developments and the new road program. The question is whether, owing to the fact that its labor is better paid and cared for, it will be able to withstand price-cutting competition from Indonesia and Malaya.

These problems are not faced by the gold and diamond miners, for gold is in constant demand and the diamond market is prevented from reaching a saturation point by artificial controls. Cobalt is still virtually a Congolese monopoly, and the production of other minerals can be geared to the requirements of the world market. Are copper and tin mining eventually to be subsidized at the expense of other enterprises which are not faced by cut-throat competition? There was much talk of this when I was last in the Belgian Congo, but somehow I don't think such a step will become necessary.

Apart from uranium, which is still mentioned in conspiratorial whispers in the clubs and taverns of Leopoldville and Elizabethville—though, goodness knows, we are all aware that the Congo produces all sorts of radioactive metals—there is radium. Radium is mined in the open at a place called Shinkolobwe in the Katanga, where it is found associated with uranium. The pitchblende radium ore is shipped to Oolen, in Belgium, where some sixty grams, just over two ounces, are extracted each year. Little as this may seem, the Congo enjoyed a practical monopoly in radium production from 1921, when exploitation began, until 1933 when richer deposits were located in Canada.

8

Ruanda-Urundi

ROADS LEAD from the Katanga southward into British territory, eastward to the prosperous settlements on the shore of Lake Tanganyika and northward through Uvira to Ruanda-Urundi, which is not, as many think, an appendage to the Belgian Congo but a separately administered trusteeship territory mandated to Belgium following the collapse of the German Empire in East Africa in the First World War.

This mountainous region, well settled, growing slowly more economically balanced, and climatically suited for European settlement, is bordered on the west by Belgian Congo territory and the shores of Lake Kivu and Lake Tanganyika and on the north and east by British East Africa. Divided from north to south by the Congo-Nile ridge, which forms a barrier of mountains near its western boundary, the greater part of Ruanda-Urundi is included in the Nile basin. This fact has no doubt influenced the migrations which are responsible for the racial peculiarities that set this area apart.

Ruanda-Urundi is the land of the giants. These tall black aristocrats, who average six feet six inches in height and whose athletes can leap over eight feet into the air, are strangers from the north. The Tusi, Batutsi, Watusi as they are variously called, and the Warundi, who now lord it over the Bantu tribes and the pygmoids of Ruanda and Urundi, are Hamites, of the same stock—so it is generally believed—as the ancient Egyptians. Venerating the cow as their forebears adored the bull Apis and the cow-goddess Hathor, these people, pushed south by Arab invaders, moved slowly toward the equator. Driving before them their strange cattle with the spreading lyre-shaped horns, exhausting the pasture as they went, they founded powerful kingdoms in their successive migrations, coming at last to the cool pastures of Ruanda some five hundred years ago.

Here they found a primitive Bantu people, the Bahutu, and the Batwa pygmoids; and being wealthier, more intelligent, taller and more vigorous, they soon took over and have remained rulers ever since. Although they are outnumbered by the Bantu peoples and the Batwa by as much as eight to one, the Batutsi have experienced little difficulty in maintaining their supremacy, since they have what to the Bahutu and the Batwa is the all-important source of wealth—the possession of 1,000,000 head of cattle.

The very first act of these warrior herdsmen after their successful penetration into the southern highlands was to prohibit their underlings from keeping cattle, which the Negro tribes would have given up anything—even their liberty—to possess. The enslavement of the Bahutu was completed by an involved process of lease-lend, under which cattle were entrusted to their care in return for regular services of many kinds.

Such was the situation when the Germans added Ruanda-Urundi to their African Empire. Although Bismarck's envoys were not noted for their clemency toward the natives, they were more interested in commercial exploitation than in upsetting the established social system. Thus, when Belgium assumed the League of Nations mandate for Ruanda-Urundi in October 1924 her administrators came face to face with a system which had been little modified, if at all, by Prussianization. Impressed by what they found and wisely taking note of the firm foundation on which this racial-*cum*-caste organization was constructed, the Belgians have never sought to make any drastic changes. They have an ace in the hole in that the antiquated economic system is bound to break down as European influence continues to increase, and they are preparing for this day by creating a number of economic cushions.

The Batutsi are the heirs of a culture as old as Osiris, but that does not mean they have developed any special aptitude for government. Their coming brought a succession of wars, and the demands of the Batutsi victors were not always tempered with mercy. The stern, repressive measures applied by the Germans on the slightest provocation kept the country in a state of uneasy peace:

the coming of a more liberal Belgian administration encouraged the Batutsi to try their hand at rebellion with
the result that the Mwami (Sultan) Musinga was deposed
and his ritual drums impounded. The trouble ceased
almost the same day and the new ruler, Mutara III, has
proved that, although capable of independent action, he
is a loyal supporter of the trusteeship agreement.

The royal drums of Ruanda, like those of many African native kingdoms, are part and parcel of the everyday life of the people. They are a call to worship, play
or work. In Ruanda-Urundi and the kingdoms of Ankole
and Buganda they were until quite recently infinitely
more: they were the very symbol of majesty.

The small native kingdom of Ankole in British Uganda
has drums of white hide, decorated with a black band.
The white tops seem to glow in the shade of the royal hut
like two immense eyes surveying the realm. When a new
king comes to the throne the skins are replaced by fresh
ones which have been washed in human blood—nowadays voluntarily given, or so we are assured—both as a
charm and an indication of the change.

In Ruanda the Karinga drum, the emblem of power,
was supposed to contain the soul of the king. It accompanied him everywhere and was entitled to the same de-
ference as he was; from time to time it was anointed with
bull's blood to bring strength to the Mwami and victory
for his arms. In times of war it rallied the feudal chiefs
and the corpses of vanquished enemy kings were tied by
ropes to its rim in token of subjection and enslavement.
In days of peace Karinga was kept in an anointed case

along with the lesser ritual drums and trophies of the
victories of these Hamite kings over the aboriginal
princes.

Yet, according to tradition, the Karinga is not itself
of Batutsi origin. It was supposedly taken from a Bantu
king of the Great Lakes about 400 years ago and was at
first kept merely as booty. The Batutsi were at that time
newcomers to the region, but as they mixed more and
more with the peoples of Ruanda and Urundi, they
adopted some of the beliefs, customs and languages (the
word "Mwami" itself is taken from a Bantu dialect) of
the country. Gradually the drums were surrounded
with ritual and clothed with supernatural power. Until
two decades ago they had never been challenged.

The guardians of war trophies were always chosen
from the Abiru clan, a family group which, like the
Levites of the Old Testament, had the task of preserving
the law and traditions of the people. It was among the
duties of the Abiru to shield the drums from the designs
of would-be usurpers, for had they been defiled, the
monarchy would have fallen and anarchy would have
reigned. When the Mwami went forth on a punitive
expedition, Karinga went with him, jealously watched
over by its Abiru bodyguard. With the armies went three
other drums, Ishakwe, Inyahura and Inumva, whose
names symbolized "My Lord the King is all powerful,"
"I am the Master of the Nations" and "My realm is all-
embracing."

This edifice of ritual collapsed in 1931 when Mwami
Musinga decided to test his strength against the Belgians.

He was defeated and deposed, and the drums were appropriated by the Belgian Deputy Governor-General and taken to Nyanza in upper Ruanda-Urandi (they were wisely kept within the territory) where they were impounded until the situation returned to normal. With their emblems of power taken away the rebellious spirits were soon silenced, and Karinga and its companions were restored, their prestige unimpaired, when Mutara III came to the throne.

These and other drums now beat out the passing of the days. They have different names. There is 'Ndamutsa, the Voice of Welcome, which has the privilege of awakening the Mwami each morning, for by tradition he cannot awaken to the song of the birds. There is Urubunda, which calls the chieftains to council, and there is the battery which gives the signal for the cattle to leave the kraals at the break of day. Yes, each drumbeat is still a note of authority, a sounding witness of the lordship of the Batutsi herdsmen over the land.

When the Europeans came they found the Mwami at the apex of a complex hierarchy: he was the eminent proprietor, the supreme dispenser of justice, fashioned in the image of Imana, God, his father. His people called him Nyagasani, "Lord ever just, good and magnificent." Nowadays, shorn of supreme power and most of the trappings of his court, the Mwami has only his 'Ntore dancers to keep alive the memories of former glories.

The 'Ntore, the ballet dancers of the Sultan, were from time immemorial the pages of the court. All of them the sons of chieftains and notables, they had the advantages of superior education and were taught ritual and symbolic dances to charm the leisure of the monarch. The 'Ntore were instructed in the social graces and were taught politics, law and the science of war in preparation for the time when they would assume the responsibilities of their fathers.

The 'Ntore dances form a complete ballet. Formerly called "The Lance," "The Bow" and "The Shield," the steps, for no good reason that I can see, now have more peaceful names; yet the way the dancers vie with one another and the gestures they strike still show the warlike origin of the symbolism in these ballets. For their exhibitions, which they often give in public before large crowds of sight-seers, the 'Ntore wear either a short skirt with a flowered pattern or a leopard skin wrapped around the waist. Pearl straps are crossed over their breasts, and their heads are adorned with lavish headdresses of white monkey fur. Their ankles are often encircled with bells, and bows, lances or raffia-decorated sticks are carried according to the nature of the dance they are performing.

Like so many things of our time the 'Ntore dances are becoming tainted with commercialism: they are a brilliant veneer over the life of a people who go quietly about their daily business, ever looking over their shoulders at the stalking specter of economic crisis. It is a crisis of their own making, for the Belgian franc is only very slowly ousting cattle as the real currency in Ruanda-Urundi; and, following the precept of their Batutsi masters, the Bahutu and the Batwa also have come to regard cattle as a sign of wealth. But this is a wealth unrelated to economic prosperity, for until recent years few, if any, of the cattle were killed for meat, and the semiarid pasture land of the country is incapable of maintaining the vast herds, to say nothing of 2,000,000 sheep and goats which feed upon it at all seasons of the year. A serious economic predicament is arising, and the Belgians are aware that so firmly rooted is the cattle tradition that only by riding roughshod over the customs of centuries can they find a rapid solution. And to use drastic methods would be inviting troubles similar to those being experienced in other parts of the continent.

The Communists have already made a great play before the United Nations about conditions in the mandated territories and have singled out economic conditions in Ruanda-Urundi as an example of what can happen when a mandatory power shows no sense of responsibility. Their propaganda line, aimed specifically at stirring up unrest among nonself-governing peoples, makes no mention of the fact that it is just because native prejudices are so strong and because, short of drastic methods, it will take years to bring these backward economies into line with those of more advanced nations that these crises have arisen in Ruanda-Urundi and elsewhere.

In the case of Ruanda-Urundi it is something which the Batutsi cannot, or will not, see themselves. To them the number of cattle, and not the quality of the individual beast, reflects a man's wealth. As a result 980,000 head of cattle are being reared on an average of four and a half acres a beast, whereas soil economists point out that seven acres is a minimum for the type of land found in this part of Central Africa. The excess of cattle has risen to about 450,000 animals; and while the gross increase is about 120,000 a year, less than 90,000 are being written off annually.

The herds must be greatly reduced in size before the strain can be improved and the embryo cattle business of the country be put on a remunerative basis. Belgian veterinary experts are working seven days a week to overcome the apathy of the native stock raisers with regard to this and other pressing questions, and although the latest report shows that some progress is being made and a process of elimination of the sterile and degenerate animals is slowly getting under way, it may be years, given peace, before the new schemes begin to pay off visibly.

However, the methods being employed are practically painless and are necessary in view of the delicate situation in surrounding colonies. The Belgian authorities want to see the herdsman give way to the general farmer, and there are already native cultivators making a good living growing maize, coffee and cotton which they can sell for imported goods.

There is also the beginning of a tendency for commerce to pass out of the hands of Indian and Afro-Greek traders—some of whom are none too scrupulous—into the hands of Africans. This is especially true in the British colonies, although in Ruanda-Urundi native-owned businesses and co-operatives will soon attain the hundred mark, a trend which the Belgians are encouraging by leasing building space to Africans at a mere fraction of the prices being charged to Europeans and Asians. This is a retarded country, but there are encouraging signs that a native middle class is coming into being, and if it can be nursed along, it may well be that this group will be the mainstay of a new social and economic order in Ruanda-Urundi.

9

South Africa

THE INITIAL carving-up of East Africa by the powers was achieved without resort to war. Britain and France were first in the field, though later France, apart from interesting herself in Madagascar and trying to extend her influence across the Sudan to the Red Sea, confined her activities to North and West Africa. Belgium, a small power, made no efforts to push her claims beyond the Congo, where many thought at that time she had already bitten off more than she could digest. Germany and Italy were not unified states until over two thirds of the nineteenth century had passed. They came late into the colonial race, but finished with better than consolation prizes.

The history of Central Africa is the story of four men—Cecil Rhodes, Henry Morton Stanley, David Livingstone and Count Savorgnan de Brazza. Of these four Rhodes and Stanley, more flamboyant, are generally better known. But De Brazza, working south from the

Sahara, secured for France the lion's share of west-central Africa as far as the north bank of the Congo, while David Livingstone, although primarily a missionary, undertook a voyage of exploration for the Royal Geographic Society in London and showed true Scottish shrewdness when he sponsored the African Lakes Corporation, a society formed to counter Arab influence in the hitherto unexplored regions around Lake Nyasa. In 1918 the German Empire disappeared. Kaiser Wilhelm's African territories were divided among Britain, which took Tanganyika; Belgium, which assumed the Ruanda-Urundi mandate; Portugal, which was given the 400-square-mile area of Kionga—now part of the Portuguese colony of Mozambique—and the Union of South Africa, which became the trustee for Southwest Africa.

British influence still extends from Suez to the Cape, but Great Britain, because of the uneven pace of development in her several colonies and because of the obligations the new conception of commonwealth carries with it, is today in the difficult position of one teacher who is trying to run separate streams of advanced, normal and retarded children through a school at the same time. Fears are growing, and these include my own, that the task is too much for any *one* nation in today's changing world.

Recently the newspapers of several countries have been referring at great length to what they are pleased to call the "middle of the road" British policy in Africa. This vague phrase can be taken as meaning that Great Britain, in pursuance of her dream of creating a commonwealth stronghold in Africa, is willing to educate her Bantu and other non-European peoples as quickly as can be compatible with thoroughness, to the point where they can share and, as far as their specific interests are concerned, take the lead in the administration of African territories.

A laudable, though time-consuming ideal. But native nationalisms, encouraged by Communists in Central Africa and thriving on repression in South Africa, have already succeeded in fomenting unrest. Have the British time to carry through their declared colonial policies and yet avoid serious trouble?

Superficially at any rate the problem of Kenya is less involved than that posed by the British government's decision to federate the Central African territories of Northern and Southern Rhodesia and Nyasaland. The Southern Rhodesian referendum on this question ended in favor of federation, and as I write this project is materializing. But I feel—and I am supported by abundant evidence—that federation will lead to widespread discontent and will serve only to increase the distrust with which African tribesmen are already viewing the activities of the British government. We know that subversionists even now are working with some success, particularly among Rhodesian laborers in the copper belt near the border of the Belgian Congo.

Yet Great Britain, by appearing to conciliate native politicians in other parts of Africa, notably in the Gold Coast and Nigeria, has presented the South African nationalists with additional excuses for pushing their republican policies and has placed herself in a fix which

has been made all the more awkward by the return of
Doctor Malan to power in South Africa.

Britain's difficulties in South Africa go back into the
early part of the last century. More recently the liberal
policies of pro-British governments in South Africa have
failed, through lack of positive action, to arrest the swing
to extreme nationalism which had begun before the death
of General Smuts. Germanophiles and Nazis in the
former German colony of Southwest Africa were allowed by hesitant governments to thrive and spread their
doctrines right up to the eve of Hitler's war. Germans
in East Africa were doing the same thing.

"Damn fine farmers, those Germans," said the British
soldier-settler in East Africa. "Soldiers and gentlemen,
too; know how to keep the blacks in order." But never,
never a word had he to say of the Nazi Bunds and the gau-
leiters who had already been appointed against the day of
Hitler's victory. Hitler did not win his war, but Southwest Africa still has many unrepentant Nazis. Ideolog-
ically attracted by Doctor Malan's theories of white
supremacy and complete racial segregation, these people
have encouraged the South African nationalists to defy
the United Nations in debates on the future of their bar-
ren, foggy land. The seeds of the present ugly situation
were sown well over a hundred years ago; matters were
allowed to worsen at the turn of the century, when a
much firmer imperial policy—quite in keeping with the
spirit of the age—would in my pro-British opinion have
been the means to a justifiable end.

The Portuguese navigators of the latter part of the fifteenth century knew the Cape of Good Hope as *Cabo Tormentoso*, the Cape of Storms. Bartolomeu Dias rounded the Cape in 1486. Vasco da Gama, bound for Cathay, followed him in 1497. But *Cabo Tormentoso* remained only a landmark until competition for Asiatic trade brought the English and the Dutch to South Africa. Jan van Riebeek established a trading station there for the Dutch East India Company in 1652; this became the first permanent white settlement. Then came French Calvinist Protestants, fleeing their homeland after Louis XIV in 1685 revoked the Edict of Nantes which had given freedom of worship to the Huguenots. Voyagers to the Indies brought back Indonesians and Malays who mingled with the natives forming the "Cape-Colored" element. The British seized the Cape Colony in order to "protect" it against the French during the Napoleonic Wars. They restored the Cape to Holland during the breathing space afforded by the short-lived Treaty of Amiens in 1802, but began a new occupation in 1814 on the disintegration of Napoleon's Empire, leaving the Dutch settlers with a feeling of betrayal to add to their wartime humiliation.

From the very beginning this unhappy country has had a checkered background. The establishment of British rule brought no improvement, and it was not long before both British and Dutch settlers, still at variance among themselves, were alike at loggerheads with the colonial government. In the middle 1830s came the emancipation of the slaves within the British dominions.

The Dutch element, harassed by the frequent Kaffir wars and rendered despondent by what they thought was inadequate financial compensation for the serfs they had been forced to liberate by a London government with no understanding of farming conditions in Africa, set out under Piet Retief, crossed the Orange River and established independent republics.

These Boers (a Dutch word meaning peasant farmers), who whether rightly or wrongly gave such trouble to the colonial government, who gave the trained British regulars a series of sound tactical lessons in the South African War and whose descendants are now doing everything they can to prize South Africa away from the British Commonwealth, today are building up the greatest stumbling block to the peaceable settlement of *all* the African questions. These strange embittered people have had a raw deal from history: successive colonial administrations of city-bred Anglicans have failed completely to understand the fanatically Calvinistic peasant. It is true that the Boers were slave owners, and it is undoubtedly true that they were at times brutal and harsh, as are all pioneers when faced with obstacles to their progress. On the other hand the writings of Anglican missionaries, notably a Doctor Philip of the London Missionary Society at Cape Town, were heavy with bitter anti-Boer sentiment and created an unhappy prejudice against the Dutch farmers. This was all the more unfortunate since the Kaffirs—from the Arabic *kafir*, an infidel—were far from being innocent and inoffensive victims of the white man's greed. They were virile, ag-

gressive and bloodthirsty. Unaccustomed to peace among
themselves, they asked no quarter nor gave any to the
white intruders, whether English or Dutch. Thus, faced
with hostility on all sides, the forebears of today's Afrikaners felt that their rights as people trying to make their
own way in a new land were being sunk in a welter of
unsympathetic legislation.

The European peasant anywhere is a shrewd being,
and the Boers were no exception; their peasant distrust
of foreigners was heightened to xenophobia by their
leaders, especially the preachers, whose uncompromising
Calvinism had long ago destroyed their sense of proportion. Protestant fanaticism became political fanaticism.
They withdrew from the Cape to Natal to nurse their
grievances, but the British Crown annexed the new Boer
Republic of Natalia in 1843. The unhappy wanderers
settled down again in the dusty wilderness to the north
of the Orange River where, living patriarchal lives in
quiet pastoral surroundings, they tended their flocks, read
their Bibles and raised large families, never losing sight of
their dream: *Afrika voor de Afrikaners*—Africa for the
predestined Dutch settlers. The Boers have never for-
given, never forgotten.

Africa from the Cape to Nyasaland still bears the
stamp of the English parson's son, Cecil John Rhodes,
who came near to holding the wild new continent from
the Cape to the Zambezi and beyond in the palm of his
hand, and whose paling shade still hovers over its copper,
gold and diamond fields. Rhodes was born just 100 years
ago. For more than fifty of those years he has been dead:

at thirty-two he was a nonentity, at forty-four he fell from grace, at forty-nine he lay dead in a cottage on the South African shore.

This colossus, who becomes all the more gigantic when we ponder the fact that he achieved what he did in little more than the span of a childhood, has been called the last of the adventurers, the first of the fascists, an imperialistic fanatic, the most visionary of all men of business. It is true that his character was as complex as these descriptions, each fitting to some extent, would make it seem. Yet today he is threatened with eclipse; he is being outshone by the resurrected star of a stubborn old Boer farmer, Stephanus Johannes Paulus Kruger—Oom Paul—a patriarchal old bigot whose uncomplicated philosophy was circumscribed by the Old Testament and backed up by a well-oiled rifle.

Rhodes, strictly brought up in the early Victorian bourgeois piety of an English parsonage, came to have little use for the Bible beyond using a selection of its texts as a code during the conspiratorial period before the South African War. He once said that there was only a "fifty-fifty chance" that God exists. It is surprising, as Stuart Cloete so aptly puts it, "that, considering the world as a joint-stock company, he did not say there was a forty-nine per cent chance in the existence of God, which would have given him [Rhodes] control." For Rhodes was big business personified. Always a sickly boy, he was sent out to South Africa in the belief that his health would benefit and joined his brother on a Natal cotton plantation in 1869. But two years before this diamonds had been discovered on the farms of Boer homesteaders in the Transvaal near Kimberley, and, impatient of routine work on a plantation, the brothers set out in 1871 to join in the rush for riches. They made immediate strikes, and when in 1873 a barrel of liquor burst into flames, killing Rhodes's brother, Cecil went on alone to pile up a huge fortune. By 1880 he had become the dictator of the diamond fields. After urging small claimants to amalgamate, he made it his practice to buy up the mergered interests. When a man was too big to be bought and too smart to be outmaneuvered, Rhodes, by outlining to him further schemes—grandiose beyond the conception of all but himself—eliminated his potential rival by coming to terms which were always in Rhodes's favor. He was an adept at bribery and was able to name a whole string of horses after the men he had suborned. He wheedled, cajoled, flattered and played on the weaknesses and aspirations of his rivals until only two were left—the Jewish financiers Alfred Biet and Barney Barnato. He "bought" Barney Barnato, a shrewd little cockney who had arrived on the African scene with little more than a handful of cigars, by "making a gentleman of him" and securing admittance to the exclusive Kimberley Club for him. When Rhodes was unable to find any Achilles' heel in Alfred Biet, a wily operator from Hamburg, he amalgamated with him. The DeBeers' diamond trust which Rhodes and his associates formed still controls the world's diamond markets.

But long before Rhodes began to make money he began to dream. By the time he was halfway to his fortune

he had conceived a plan for the domination of the world
by the English-speaking and Teutonic peoples, who, he
thought, were those most fitted to bring the remainder
of mankind into the light of civilization. As his fortune
mounted, the plan began to take shape, the outline of his
schedule began to form: the timetable was being con-
solidated in terms of years. Money for its own sake,
which had never been an obsession with him—if it had
been he could hardly have been called really great—
gradually came to be identified with Empire. It was to
the realization of his plan for a world ruled by British
communities or communities subscribing to British ideals
that all his skill as a financier, all his persuasive talents and
all his fanaticism were directed.

North of Kimberley lay the lands of the Matabele and
the Mashona, the giant Zambezi River, the Mountains of
the Moon; far beyond the northern sky line the Nile
flowed through the Sudan and Egypt to the Mediterranean. Africa was to be painted British red from the
Cape to Alexandria; the English-speaking peoples were
to put a girdle round the earth. Rhodes even dreamed
of the return of America to the British fold. His chauvin-
ism stimulated the jingoists. Kipling sang for him, his
name was respectfully lisped in Whitehall, he was the
idol of London bus drivers and servant girls. What did it
matter that cautious old Gladstone foresaw trouble in
Rhodes's unbridled imperialism and castigated the methods of a man who had harnessed Mammon into the service
of Queen Victoria?

Behind the façade of flag waving and patriotic hymn

singing Rhodes worked every minute with deadly seriousness. In 1880 he entered politics. He rose quickly in the Cape Legislature; and the year 1891 saw him as prime minister and virtual dictator of Cape Colony, pursuing a policy which, although it restricted the franchise to literates, was liberal toward the African and the halfbreed and enjoyed the support of the more enlightened elements among the Dutch settlers of the Cape.

But, though Rhodes did not know it, the seeds of his downfall were already germinating. They had been set in 1836, the year of the great trek of the Boer farmers. Hating the British, who had decreed the liberation of their slaves, had tried to make them pay taxes—yes, had even tried to force education on them when everything they needed to know was in the Bible—the Krugers, the Retiefs, the Steenkamps, the Potgieters and the rest inspanned their oxen and set off to find freedom in the uncharted north. The stories of this *voortrekker* exodus— of the many days when the travelers moved only two miles or often none at all, of the crossing of mountain ranges, swollen rivers and sunburned plains, of the thefts of their cattle and the killing of their young and brave by painted savages—can find few parallels in modern times.

With the main party was a boy of eleven, Paul Kruger. A typical offspring of his race, he was a sturdy, even heavily built lad, a horseman from his babyhood and as strong as the horse he rode. Paul had but three months' formal schooling in his life and that at the hands of the *voortrekker* dominie, whose own academic achievements were bounded by a knowledge of "figuring" and the word according to John Calvin. The Krugers belonged to the Doppers—the "Extinguishers"—a sect of the Dutch Reformed Church noted for its hatred of innovation. Even hymns were too worldly for them. The Bible, particularly the Old Testament, contained all that was necessary for salvation. Obsessed by Calvin's doctrine of predestination, Paul grew up like the rest of his people, instinctively comparing his own kin with the Chosen People who had come out of Egypt; the Bantu tribes were the Canaanites whom it was their appointed task to enslave or destroy. The British power was Pharaoh, and it became the dream of Kruger's heart to make South Africa Dutch and to drive the British into the sea.

The great trek brought the Boers north of the Orange River to what became the Orange Free State and on across the Vaal, the great tributary of the Orange, to what they always insisted was the South African Republic, for the Boers detested the word "Transvaal." The Orange Free State drew off the more liberal and less adventurous elements among the Boers. This group did not wish to be completely cut off from the Cape government and at all times continued to maintain courteous, if somewhat cold relations with the British administration. But the *intransigeants* went on across the Vaal, driven by their urge for the open wilds where they would be free from British domination forever. Here they established their South African Republic, squatting in the territory of hostile natives and laying out their vast farms, dwellers in a land which they considered overcrowded if they could see the smoke from their neighbors' stacks.

The early years of the Transvaalers were years of

blood and sweat. They farmed against the most unfavorable odds: they suffered drought, crop and animal pests
and Zulu raids, until in 1877 the situation grew so bad
that they had to be rescued from imminent massacre at
the hands of the Zulus. The British government's subsequent annexation of the Transvaal for its own protection
increased the resentment of the Boers, and although local
autonomy was again granted in 1881 there were no signs
of gratitude, for, never given to spontaneous demonstrations of joy, these people had become even more soured
by their recent experiences and asked for nothing more
than to be allowed to withdraw into their shells. But they
had not lost sight of their fondest dream, *Afrika voor de
Afrikaners*.

In 1886, when Kruger was fifty-one years old, gold was
discovered on the Witwatersrand, the Ridge of White
Waters, the clean, wind-swept high veld 6,000 feet above
sea level where Johannesburg stands today. And from
that moment the cause of peace in South Africa was lost.
For with the finding of gold came the diggers, some honest, some slippery, all too many of them thugs and crim-
inals. In their wake came traders, tricksters, bunko boys
and whores. In the space of a few months the patriarchal
Boer farmer was brought face to face for the first time
with a new kind of violence. The violence of the Zulus
he could understand and cope with; the brutal, noisy,
drunken, vicious violence of the mining camps where the
favors of diseased women were bought with gold nuggets
and a case of champagne thrown in to clinch the deal
was something beyond him.

At this time the South African Republic was, as usual,

almost bankrupt; it was proving difficult to pay the president his meager salary. Now, thought the perplexed Boers, they would have markets for their produce; their cattle would supply the new butchers' shops, their mealies and vegetables would find eager buyers. Had they known what lay ahead they would have preferred the desperate privations of preboom days.

So Johannesburg, the city built on gold, grew up. Order began to replace the money-madness and the brutal and licentious goings on of the first days on the Rand. But Paul Kruger, now the president of the South African Republic—Oom Paul, the uncle of his people and more farsighted than most of them—perceived the new dangers in the making. The newcomers were building the cities, cutting the roads and the railways across the veld while the Boer sat on his stoep in the cool Transvaal evenings, smoking black tobacco while his wife and family took turns reading aloud from the Bible.

The newcomers were making the Transvaal prosperous for the first time in its history, and the parvenu elite among them were beginning to show their contempt for the seemingly slow-witted, ponderous white peasant beneath whose soil the source of their riches lay. These *Uitlanders*—Outsiders—as the Boers called them, soon became as numerous as the farmers and by 1885 there were 85,000 *Uitlanders* to 65,000 Boers in the South African Republic. Kruger saw the threat behind this situation and tried to avert it by excluding the non-Boers from political rights and the franchise. Ironically, there is a great deal of evidence to show that the *Uitlanders*, caring only for wealth and the vulgar ostentation in which it permitted them to indulge, worried little about the franchise. But Kruger's autocratic restriction was capital for the Cape Town government, which pretended to see in this stubborn old farmer an obstacle to any plans for northward expansion.

Rhodes, who while he was riding high was playing politics with the skill of a poker champion, was not nearly so concerned as he allowed it to be thought. His protests were made with tongue in purple-veined cheek, for he saw that it would be easy to by-pass the South African Republic and that new British territories stretching up into the heart of Africa would leave the Transvaal surrounded. But he could not resist this opportunity of embarrassing the Boers by making political capital out of their treatment of the *Uitlanders*. These adventurers were by no means all British; they represented all races, and far from wishing to become British subjects many of them, particularly the Americans in this motley throng, objected to the adoption of the Union Jack and dreamed of a Transvaal state with complete independence.

That is probably why the Jameson Raid failed. Doctor Leander Starr Jameson—"Dr. Jim" as Rhodes affectionately called him—was at the time of the *Uitlander* crisis administrator of Rhodes's colonial-*cum*-business enterprise in the lands of the Mashona and the Matabele in what is now Rhodesia. "Dr. Jim," whom Rhodes loved as a brother, yet who was destined to be his evil genius, organized a foray into the Transvaal with the object of linking up with fellow conspirators in Johan-

nesburg and forcing a redress of the *Uitlanders'* loudly
publicized grievances. But as a result of a combination
of bad staff work and apathy the Johannesburgers failed
to play their part, and Jameson and his 600 men, many
of them addlepated young British Army officers, were
quickly overcome, rounded up and hauled off to ig-
nominious captivity. Rhodes, against his own better
judgment, had been party to Jameson's ridiculous gesture.
As a military operation the skirmish was negligible, but
the howl of public indignation (or more likely morti-
fication) in Britain toppled Rhodes from power. He
resigned amid the uproar and left the political stage forever.

Kruger treated the incident with contempt. In fact he
publicly ignored it, though he had some very acid private
comment reserved for the prisoners. The failure of this
unhappy privateering venture had raised Kruger's stock
a good many points and representations by the British
government in favor of the *Uitlanders* met with a stubborn silence. Oom Paul was hanging grimly on to his
precious Transvaal, the cradle of his schemes for an
Afrikander South Africa. A concession of the franchise
to the *Uitlanders* at this point would have been tanta-
mount to a resignation on his part, so he defied the British
Empire and turned a deaf ear to the mounting clamor of
the jingoists in London and Cape Town. Kruger should
have seen the Jameson raid for what it was, a flag-wag-
ging *demarche*, but none the less a straw in the wind. He
dismissed it at its face value—a military fiasco—and refused to see any significance in the revenge-crazed clamor

of the British mob. Thus it was inevitable that the situation should drift toward war. And when war came the British, in spite of some humiliating defeats and many object lessons in tactics and strategy at the hands of the gallant farmers, succeeded in crushing the Boers and destroying their republic. The South African, or Boer, War lasted until 1902, and altogether the British had to put 450,000 men into the field against 66,000 well-disciplined and fanatical Boers.

Then came peace and the reconstruction of South Africa. The British terms were generous and were aimed at placating the Dutch. In return for their recognition of Edward VII as King of South Africa they were offered 3,000,000 pounds (at that time $15,000,000) to repair farm destruction, their language was recognized as one of South Africa's two official languages, they were promised self-government, an amnesty was declared for legitimate acts of war and it was agreed that landed property should not be subjected to a tax to pay war costs. In 1910 Cape Province, Natal and the former territory of the Dutch republics were unified, and in an attempt to please all sections of the population Pretoria—named after the first president of the South African Republic, Marthinus Pretorius—was made the seat of the government; Bloemfontein became the center of the judiciary, and the parliament building was established at Cape Town. The first prime minister of this newly founded Union of South Africa was Louis Botha, the victorious Boer leader of the South African War's Battle of Colenso: in his cabinet was young Jan Christiaan

Smuts, later to become the outstanding military and political figure of South African history.

Thus ended the era of Rhodes and Kruger. By the end
of the South African War Rhodes had died of consumption; Kruger was soon to die in bitter exile in Switzer-
land. Rhodes, the misogynist, the businessman-visionary,
who stalked the diamond fields with a Greek lexicon in
his pocket. Rhodes, who tried to buy Africa and every-
body in it, yet did not want it for himself, but for Britain.
He was an imperialistic fanatic and wealth was the means
to the creation of his empire. Loyal to his friends, generous to his foes, the most persuasive of orators, as polished as his finest diamonds. Rhodes, the shabbily dressed
multimillionaire who built Groote Schuur near Cape
Town, a solid, somber mansion—a man's house, with a
man's library, a man's furniture and no concession to
femininity.

Rhodes and Kruger were both big men, but Kruger
was more rugged. Kruger limped, having broken a leg
when his ox wagon turned over on him; he had lost part
of a thumb, shattered in a hunting accident. (He cut off
the top joint himself and dipped the gangrenous wound
into the boiling entrails of a goat.) Rhodes could sit up
all night and drink champagne if he saw a business deal
in the offing; Kruger saw liquor as second only to gold
and diamonds in the devil's arsenal. Rhodes permitted
self-criticism. Kruger could not do so, for every decision
he made was inspired by Biblical instance or precept; and
since in his eyes the Bible could never be wrong, then
neither could Kruger. Kruger, with a rifle across his

knees, his hand on the Bible and his meerschaum in his mouth, despised everything Rhodes stood for. Rhodes, more tolerant, respected the integrity of the man he never succeeded in buying, though he was hopeful to the last of making a deal with Kruger. Nor did he underestimate Kruger and the Dutch. Shortly before he died, when there was great rejoicing in England and among the British at the Cape over what seemed to be the crippling blow struck at the Boers (in actual fact the defeats suffered by the Boer armies were the prelude to a costly guerilla war), Rhodes said: "You may think you have beaten the Dutch. It is not so. The Dutch are not beaten. What is beaten is Krugerism, a corrupt and evil government, no more Dutch in essence than English. No! The Dutch are as vigorous and unconquered today as they ever have been. The country is still as much theirs as yours, and you will have to live and work with them hereafter as in the past."

But Rhodes was wrong in assuming that Krugerism was dead. Incapable of intense religious convictions himself, he did not take sufficiently into account the way in which literal interpretations of the Bible can be harnessed to an ideal.[1] Krugerism, even in the '80s a political anach-

---

[1] "And [Noah] said, Cursed be Canaan [the son of Ham]; a servant of servants shall he be unto his brethren. And he said, blessed be the Lord God of Shem; and Canaan shall be his servant. God shall enlarge Japheth, and he shall dwell in the tents of Shem; and Canaan shall be his servant."

(The reference to the subjection of the Hamites is clear, but I find it difficult to reconcile the reference to Shem with the anti-Semitism of the Malanists.)

ronism, despised the unrestricted use of wealth as a means to government; Malanism, a more dangerous anachronism, has compromised with Mammon. There can be no compromise between Malan's plan for a human zoo and liberal ideals. Reaction is triumphant, and it is still backed by that Calvinistic fanaticism which drove the *voortrekkers* north 127 years ago.

10

South Africa (Continued)

THE PRESENT British predicament not only in South Africa but throughout Britain's African territories can only be understood against the patchwork quilt of South Africa's uneasy political history. Since the Treaty of Vereeniging, which ended the Boer War in 1902, was unrealistic in that it took no account of Afrikander ambitions, there was little hope that pacification of the country would be lasting. The problem of the Union of South Africa is unique in the continent, setting, as it does, two white races in opposition. The continually deteriorating position of the Negro in South African society and the publicity which has been given to his oppression have led the British government to employ very cautious native policies elsewhere.

The racial tension created by South African nationalist attitudes toward the native has emphasized the need for Britain to act wisely and with much careful deliberation to minimize the effects the South African situation is having in neighboring British territories. The peoples of Kenya, Uganda, Tanganyika, Nyasaland and the Rhodesias observe with anxiety the reactions of a British government embarrassed by developments within a commonwealth which supposedly worships freedom. If they begin to think, with or without incitement from disaffected or subversive sources, that any new British measure is a threat to their eventual self-determination, there will be immediate trouble. This is proved by the recent unrest in Nyasaland over the federation issue.

Meanwhile since 1902 the triangular South African problem has steadily become more acute and more complex, though two world wars have intervened to send it into temporary obscurity.

The peace of Vereeniging left many recalcitrants among the Boers. Cabinet Ministers Hertzog and De Wet, Boer leaders whose bitter tears—like those of thousands of their fellows—had never dried, broke away when Botha, to demonstrate the loyalty of the Union of South Africa, declared that future British wars would be South African wars, too. The uneasy peace continued until the outbreak of the First World War when Botha's declaration was put to the test, precipitating a Boer rebellion. The insurrection assumed all the aspects of a bitter civil war and had to be suppressed before South Africa could put troops into the field against the Germans in Southwest Africa and Tanganyika. British troops were not called in to help the loyalists for fear of worsening an already ugly situation.

Smuts became prime minister in 1919 on the death of Botha, but he made little headway against the solid core of Boer *intransigeance* in spite of concessions on the flag question (the nationalists objected to the Union Jack) and a truce with General Hertzog, the aging Boer leader.

Throughout World War II tension was high. I spent some time in both the Cape and Natal, and in both places it was easy to note the hostile attitude of sections of the South African Dutch. An English doctor with whom I was traveling in the early days of World War II was beaten up as a result of having too much to say in Durban about conscription for South African whites. He'd had a few drinks at the time, was in Royal Air Force uniform and opened his mouth very wide before a group of strangers. He was promptly shipped to Suez and his lacerations were officially attributed to his participation in a brawl in a native *shibeen*—liquor shop. I know better because I bunked with him on my way up to Aden aboard the *S/S Aronda* and he told me the whole story.

Other unfortunates beside the Negro in South Africa are the Cape-Colored population and the numerous Indians. The former, descendants of the Malays and Indonesians of the early days and mixed with white and Hottentot elements, has produced a mulatto group which for the most part lives in squalor and is ridden with disease and responsible for a high rate of crime. Nevertheless, the past twenty years have seen the birth of an "identity" for these unfortunates, and their leaders are doing a great deal to redeem them morally and materially. There are only about 100,000 of them, and Doctor Malan makes no secret of his design to withdraw the Cape-Colored franchise and replace it by a system of "separate representation." In other words the Cape-Coloreds will be represented in parliament by a spokesman, or possibly spokesmen, especially selected for this purpose.

This, then, is the unenviable inheritance of Daniel Malan, a former Calvinist minister and journalist. He is tackling South African problems with a clear-cut program and, so it would seem from his propaganda, a clear Christian conscience. It is easy to see the reasons for his actions, though it is hard to find excuses for them. The old Boer dream is not dead—*Afrika voor de Afrikaners.* The prime minister, himself an extremist, is surrounded by extremists, sons and grandsons of the men who nursed the Afrikander dream in their bitter self-imposed exile in the sparse plateau lands of the north. They see themselves approaching their Jerusalem and they will ride conscience-free over the human rights of others to get there.

Malanism is nothing new. A Mrs. Steenekamp, a descendant of Piet Retief, the leader of the great trek, wrote in 1876:

. . . the shameful and unjust proceedings with reference to the freedom of our slaves; and yet it is not so much their freedom which drove us to such lengths, as their being placed on an equal footing with Christians contrary to the law of God and the natural distinction of races and religions, so that it was intolerable for any decent Christian to bow down beneath such a yoke: wherefore we rather withdrew in order to preserve our doctrines in purity.

These words have the cold ferocity of a fanatic. The ox wagon of the Boer of today is a blundering conveyance full of race hatred and theories of racial purity and white supremacy. There is in his narrow philosophy all the armory of the fascist: there is the same old smoldering resentment of Britain and all she stands for, there is a burning hatred, tempered with scorn, for the Negroes, Indians, mulattoes and Jews. Anti-Semitic slogans and posters used in the election campaign in the spring of 1953 recalled the days of Hitler's Reich.

For the outside world, however, the Nationalists have put out a lot of specious propaganda in defense of their position. A very expensive document has been prepared in at least two languages to show how the Indian is being well treated. The book contrasts the underfed castoffs who arrived during the nineteenth century with the sleek, well-nourished Indian merchant and professional man of today. But the book confines its survey to the glossy Indian fringe and the few better aspects of the Indian employment problem. And why, if the Indian is supposed to be doing so well, is he so profoundly discontented? Why should the son of Mahatma Gandhi (himself an Indian lawyer in South Africa at one time) be playing such an active part in the campaign of civil disobedience? Manilal Gandhi has been arrested several times for defying the social color bar (which affects Indians as much as Africans). He has ridden on public transport reserved for whites; he has sat on park benches which must not be defiled by a non-European. Small instances, but aimed at a monstrous and inhuman principle.

The South African Department of Native Affairs makes great play of the educational facilities being provided for natives, pointing to the growing number of Negro intellectuals, doctors and clergy. The policy of building up reserves is being put forward as exemplary; the reclamation of land along the coasts of Zululand and Natal and the development of fruit and vegetable farming in northeastern Natal are loudly advertised. Such projects are a drop in the ocean, as the Nationalists themselves are forced to admit. Yet they protest these things too loudly for their alleged good will to be taken at its face value, even if the Native Affairs Department contains, as it undoubtedly does, many able and hard-working officers. If there is any good will toward the African at all, it could be shown by promoting the growth of a responsible native middle class which could work with, and among, the whites. Such a body could provide a stabilizing factor in the dangerous days ahead. But, no, the *apartheid* (segregation)-inspired urban-area legislation makes this impossible.

In early 1953 the United party sustained its second successive defeat at the polls. It seems within the order of things nowadays that vigorous, noisy and bullying minorities shall rule. Doctor Malan's doctrines of total race segregation and white superiority could not but appeal to his Boer followers, who had been steeped in such theories from the moment they could understand anything at all, but the wavering segment of the electorate has obviously been influenced by the South African prime minister's emotional exposé of his case during the campaign period. The technique of the velvet glove was cleverly used, and the prompt exploitation of the anti-white agitation which followed Jomo Kenyatta's prison sentence in Kenya (q.v.) brought Malan more than a few British voters. Though in 1953 the United party polled 50,000 more votes than the Malan Nationalists, the latter, because of the nonproportional system of representation, won ninety-four seats in the 159-seat House, as against eighty-six in the previous administration.

Speaking at Stellenbosch, the seat of the South African Dutch University, in early March 1953, Doctor Malan gave notice to the world at large and to South Africa in particular that if returned to power he could not, and would not, go back on one single point of his *apartheid* platform, and in addition he would press his design for the sovereignty of parliament over the judiciary—a scheme born as an outcome of the Supreme Court's rejection of some of the Malanist projects, among them the disfranchisement of the Cape Colored.

In this Stellenbosch speech, which was widely reported abroad, Malan made an attempt to justify theories which in other surroundings would have caused a political explosion. With a trained politician's eye, he made a special appeal to politically immature university students who can always be relied on to lend color to mob demonstrations. It is only eight years since the end of Hitler's war; yet here once again were the same old theories with the same trappings and tactics, selling themselves to almost fifty per cent of the voters of a nation.

Doctor Malan was greeted with Afrikaans Nationalist

songs and billboarded slogans: "You lead—Young South Africa Follows." He spoke in Afrikaans, an unwieldy language in spite of all efforts to make it a literary vehicle. But it is the language of a movement. What is more, comparatively few British South Africans, who are just about as blind to language culture as Americans, can follow exactly what is being said.

Doctor Malan made no bones about the color question: the greatest and most urgent matter on which the election must hinge, he said, was the racial problem. Between the alternatives of equality, which meant the abolition of all color discrimination, and *apartheid*, which would allow those on both sides of the barrier free development according to their capacity and level of civilization, there is no middle way. Any middle-of-the-road liberal nonsense will leave the problem unsolved, said Doctor Malan, and will provide an open invitation to the Communist agitator.

The activities of the United Nations were singled out for special treatment: "The meddlesome and aggressive United Nations, which was intended to help preserve world peace, vigorously contributed, through the creation of so-called world opinion, to arousing unrest, and even revolt, among the more primitive races." At this point in his speech Malan became somewhat more thought-provoking. Liberalistic elements, he said, had clamorously proclaimed that color discrimination in any form was inhuman suppression and had awakened an expectation among non-Europeans that even the most extravagant claims would enjoy the support of the whole world. The bitter fruits of this, he continued, had soon become noticeable, and the demand that the white man should leave Africa altogether had increased. Bloody scenes had followed in Kenya, and even within the Union organized resistance movements had led in some places to murder and death coupled with the most barbaric cruelty.

The South African prime minister went on to claim that in the *apartheid* question there were four basic facts to be considered. First, the whites have at least as much right to South Africa as the nonwhites, for both arrived from outside and at approximately the same time—he was referring to the southward migrations of the Bantu in the sixteenth century. Second, the whites who moved inland obtained their farms and holdings not by force, and much less by a process of extermination, as had happened elsewhere, but by negotiation and by settling in practically unoccupied areas. "In spite of our traducers," he said, "we have proved that we are a Christian nation." Third, the land now belonging to natives in the Union and Southwest Africa extends to 40,000 square miles and includes some of the best territory for settlement in the whole country. Finally, the whites, unlike those in some other countries inhabited by nonwhites, are in South Africa permanently. They are now a specific nation with one specific fatherland; "They must die here, with or without honor."

Some of Malan's bitterest comment was reserved for the press. English and Afrikaans-speaking groups, he said, are drawing closer together (why, then, does he

wish to abolish English as an official language?) and this
was being achieved in the face of misunderstanding and
misrepresentation abroad, threats and traducement and
in spite of an organized and hostile world press against
which the best efforts to inform outsiders were like a drop
in a bucket.

The strong-arm campaign tactics of the Nationalists
and their boisterous political meetings which sometimes
ended in riots amid cries of "Heil Hitler" made the
United party seem colorless and "me too-ish." Agreeing
that white supremacy has to be maintained in South
Africa, but advocating the employment of more humane
methods, opposition members, led by Jacobus Strauss,
voiced feeble, protesting pleas which were drowned in a
fascist wind. The "Torchlight Commando," an anti-
Malan ex-servicemen's organization led by "Sailor
Malan," a distant relative of Daniel Malan and an air ace
of the last war, promised great things for a time. Its
political immaturity and the fact that it did not admit
Africans or other nonwhites seriously weakened its appeal among Negroes and others. I fear little more will be
heard of it, though at the Commando's general rally in
June 1953 a disbandment proposal was overruled.

The statistics of the language question give no encouragement to those who would like to think that there will
be a revival in the fortunes of the United party. Census
figures show that for every 100 English-speaking persons
over twenty-one there are 115 Afrikaans speakers. For
every 100 English-speaking children over the age of

seven there are 185 Afrikaans-speaking, while of children
under seven years of age there are 212 Afrikaans to 100
English. One may be certain that these Afrikaans-speaking children are being reared in the strict Nationalist
tradition. The effect of British immigration since the end
of the war is nullified by the law which prohibits newcomers from voting for five years after their arrival. Of
the 20,000 United Kingdom immigrants who took advantage of the postwar settlement scheme only *five* had
become South Africans in time to qualify. Had all 20,-
000 been eligible to vote their voices would most probably have increased the United party's over-all majority
to 70,000, but since most of them are living in or near
cities there is little likelihood that they could have influenced the present distribution of seats in Parliament.
It is noticeable that the Boer birth rate is almost double
the British. As it was in Nazi Germany before the war,
it is the "duty" of South African Dutch mothers to have
large families in order to maintain Boer supremacy.

So, as South Africa moves toward totalitarianism,
liberal-minded elements are being forced to choose between the dispirited opposition and the nonwhite campaign of passive resistance to the government, which is
fathered by such groups as the African and Indian Con-
gresses of South Africa. These bodies, which have no
legislative authority, were formed by nonwhites (and
supported by white liberals) for the co-ordination of a
plan of campaign for the redress of grievances. One of
the greatest friends of the African, a man who sincerely

desires to see harmony restored and the colored man in a position to enjoy the fruits of living in what is, after all, his own country, has taken a stand which yet may prove the beginning of a liberal rally—if he is allowed to continue. He is Father Trevor Huddleston, priest-in-charge of the Community of the Resurrection Mission in the squalid, teeming, corrugated-iron and mud African township of Orlando, a suburb of Johannesburg. In a speech before an Indian and African Congress meeting called in protest against one of Malan's so-called public safety segregation measures, Father Huddleston identified himself completely with the Asian and African struggle for recognition. Father Huddleston, who is supposed to have inspired the character of the gentle priest in Alan Paton's *Cry the Beloved Country*, had until recently believed it his duty to refrain from political action. Now, from his newly adopted position, he states that it has been the teaching of the Christian church throughout the ages that when a government degenerates into tyranny its laws are no longer binding on its subjects. To make such a statement requires phenomenal courage, since Father Huddleston's personal opinion, however widely it may be shared, cannot be considered the official point of view of his church. The Reverend Michael Scott, who a year or two ago took up the case of the Herero people of Southwest Africa in the acrimonious United Nations debates on the future of this South African mandated territory, was unceremoniously declared *persona non grata* by the Nationalist government.

The new South African administration has already shown its teeth. The appointment of the extreme Nationalist Johannes Strydom as deputy prime minister has shattered the hopes of all those who thought that victory might be tempered with mercy. "We've been put into power in South Africa to rule forever," is the cry. Doctor Malan is an old man. He is now seventy-nine, and many think that he is grooming Strydom for the premiership. And if Strydom becomes the next leader of Boer South Africa, we can expect the worst. Already the hard-hit United party seems on the verge of disintegration. Its leaders are constantly asserting that there is no basic difference between their own and Nationalist aims and that the latter could be justified constitutionally— that is, with the support of United party votes—if Malan's men would compromise on the remaining small difficulties.[2] This acquiescence of United party leaders has caused the defection of their more liberal-minded supporters. A South African Liberal party, of which Alan Paton is one of the founders, has come into being with a charter which emphasizes the essential dignity of all hu-

----

[2] In October 1953 Doctor Malan came within reach of his two principal objectives in internal policy—the withdrawal of the direct franchise from the Cape-Colored element and a division among United party members on the color question. The Nationalists and the United party voted together to set up a joint commission on colored representation. The constitution of this body left little hope of the eventual survival of the Cape-Colored franchise, for eleven members were Nationalists, two came from other parties (including the Socialists), while five were from the right wing of the United party—a group which holds identical views with the Nationalists on the color question.

man beings, irrespective of race, creed or color, and the maintenance of their fundamental rights. As yet a tottering infant, the Liberal party will find support among liberal whites, Indians and most Africans: its handicap will lie in the fact that the greater part of its members are denied the franchise. Its voice, too, may be silenced by Nationalist legislation restricting the holding of meetings, but there is no doubt that its leaders can shape the civil-disobedience campaign into a more effective political weapon than it is at present.

The Nationalists have asserted that their first task is to crush the developing nonwhite resistance. The new government has arrogated powers to declare emergencies, suspend laws and imprison or flog persons who object too loudly to existing laws, or to decrees which may be enacted in future. Even more, the Malanists have left no doubt that they will go to the length of scrapping traditional democratic rights if they deem such action necessary to preserve the complete supremacy of South Africa's 2,500,000 whites over the 9,000,000 already underprivileged non-Europeans.

The Nationalists mean what they say. Patrick Duncan, the son of a former British governor-general of South Africa, was sentenced to 100 days' imprisonment in June 1953 for backing a protest against the eviction of 90,000 Africans from the western areas of Johannesburg under the terms of the Group Areas (Segregation) Act. Duncan also attacked the government for doing nothing to house the 50,000 African workers on the waiting list for accommodations. "This cruel scheme is without parallel in history. A farmer would not treat his animals so," Mr. Duncan said.

All colored groups in South Africa, whether cultural, educational or even sporting, are now obliged to direct any requests for financial or administrative assistance to the South African government's Colored Affairs Department. As the London *Observer* pointed out some time ago, money is only granted or co-operation offered on condition the groups involved declare their attachment to the government's *apartheid* policy.

The trade-union movement also has drawn the fire of the government. Popular trade-union leaders are being expelled (usually following the farce of having them "named" under the Suppression of Communism Act) and Nationalist "yes-men" are appointed in their places. Natives' representatives in Parliament also have a rough time if they show any spark of independence. The representatives for the Cape Western constituency have twice been deposed in the last eighteen months.

In 1952 the United National General Assembly set up a commission to consider the question of the increased racial tension in South Africa resulting from Malan's segregation and racial-discrimination policies. Malan promptly boycotted this commission and ever since has continued to attack the United Nations for attempting to obstruct the internal policies of a free nation. By defying the United Nations Malan has set the world by the ears. But protests are feeble, and his government will assume an even more authoritarian character by continuing blindly with reactionary theories. The tragedy of all this is that when an explosion does come, the whole of black Africa will be involved. The vengeful tide released in South Africa could easily swamp and quickly obliterate the good work which is being done in the African's behalf in other territories.

11

Central African Federation

ACROSS THE thousand-mile-long Limpopo, the Crocodile River—Rio do Espirito Santo, as it was more euphemistically called by Vasco da Gama when he discovered it in 1497—lie Bechuanaland and Southern Rhodesia. The arid plateau of Bechuanaland was annexed by Great Britain as a protectorate in 1885. Inhabited by gentle, pastoral people, this backward country is coveted by South Africa, but the Union's more pressing claims to Swaziland and Basutoland, native protectorates islanded by Union territory, have allowed the shelving of any immediate agitation for its incorporation. Bechuanaland is rarely heard from in this world of more acute problems, although it received an unflattering sort of publicity—which included wild debates in the British House of Commons—when the marriage of its hereditary ruler, Seretse Khama, to an English girl led to his banishment for what may best be described as "sociological reasons."

Southern Rhodesia, by contrast, is a country whose future is being regarded with great concern. In the early days of colonization the two Rhodesias were one territory. Administered by the South Africa Company until 1923, the portion of the country to the north of the Zambezi River became in that year the Crown Colony of Northern Rhodesia. Southern Rhodesia became a self-governing colony at the same time.

These rich lands of grain, fruit, tobacco and untold mineral resources are now included with Nyasaland in a British government scheme for the federation of her Central African territories. This highly controversial proposition has been bitterly argued for a long time, but the practical approval given in the Southern Rhodesian referendum early in 1953 encouraged the British government to go ahead with the scheme, which is now presented to the natives of the three territories as a *fait accompli*. Since Southern Rhodesia is a self-governing territory, the proposed federation could not have been imposed without sounding the opinion of the country's voters. In the case of the other two territories concerned, approval of the scheme had to be given by the British Parliament.

The result of the popular referendum in Southern Rhodesia was an almost two-thirds majority in favor of federation. But the qualifications for the franchise in Southern Rhodesia are such that only a small proportion of the total population was able to cast a vote. To become eligible to vote a native must be in possession of assets to the value of $1,400 or an income of $700 a year—almost astronomical figures in African circles. But sponsors of federation maintain that the growth of more liberal opinion among the Europeans will, for practical and ethical reasons, reduce discrimination to a point where the native will get a fair deal in social and economic matters. This I fail to see. The forty or more years during which the Union of South Africa has become steadily less liberal have had their effect on other African territories, and on Northern and Southern Rhodesia in particular. This is inevitable because, with time, the attempts of the European element to maintain itself as an aristocracy living off the labor of the African have been presented with mounting difficulties.

The Rhodesias have shown a tendency to follow the South African pattern in the imposition of color bars, particularly regarding job discrimination. Southern and Northern Rhodesia have a growing number of white artisans, and this group has been instrumental, through its unions, in keeping the African down in the lower manual-worker grades in order to prevent his competing for jobs. It has to be admitted that since the inevitability of federation has come to be assumed, there has been a move toward at least discussing the betterment of the status of the Rhodesian native worker. In the Northern Rhodesian copper belt there have been signs that an urgent plea before the Legislative Council of Northern Rhodesia in July 1953 by the governor of the territory, Sir Gilbert Rennie, has caused the leaders of the European Mineworkers Union in the copper belt to pause and consider the possible upheaval which continued discrimination may bring about. Even though this hesitancy has not, as far as I know, led to tangible proposals, it can nevertheless be taken as a sign that many Europeans within the mining industry are beginning to see that a sympathetic attitude toward African emancipation is essential if the policy of federation is to have any chance of success. There is, however, a pressing need for an easing up of discriminatory practices not only in industry, but in those little everyday pinpricks which vitiate race relationships.

In the recent referendum, because of the property and salary qualifications, only 429 Southern Rhodesian Africans and a handful of other nonwhites were eligible to vote out of a total population of nearly two million. The voting in favor of federation was 25,570 to 14,729, the opposition votes being cast for two main reasons. The few convinced liberals felt that the scheme gave too little in the way of safeguards to the natives against eventual complete white domination on the Boer pattern. The remainder actually preferred the adoption of a system based on the Nationalist policies of the Union of South Africa, though not necessarily so drastic. This minority vote was large, and should Malanism bring even superficial calm to South Africa, then there is every danger that the Rhodesian supporters of *apartheid* would organize themselves and cause a great deal of unrest within the new federated dominion. At the opposite end of the scale from this extremist fringe there is the vast native population of the three countries. Africans are opposed to federation because of what they consider to be insufficient provisions for the maintenance of freedom and dignity in the African way of life. The native Central African Congress is in vociferous opposition and its honest disapproval is being exploited by agitators whose one purpose is to perpetuate unrest. These people have been more than successful in Northern Rhodesia. While the majority of the chiefs continue to discharge their duties loyally, it was nevertheless necessary during 1953 to suspend several of them from their functions, and a certain Kasoma Bangwulu, who threatened violence to government servants, was arrested. It was also stated in a dispatch from Lusaka, the capital of Northern Rhodesia, that cases before the courts have brought to light a deterioration in race relations—a result of the increasing success of agitators in spreading rumors against the government. The pattern, now familiar enough in Kenya, is definitely emerging in the industrialized copper belt: Africans are commanded to carry out the orders of the agitators under threat of injury or death.

Harry Franklin, of the Northern Rhodesian Information Department in Lusaka, with whom I had a long talk some time ago, knows more about his Rhodesians than all the pundits of Whitehall put together. Toward the end of February 1953 and before the taking of the referendum in Southern Rhodesia, Franklin stated that while the government's action in imposing severe penalties on the recalcitrants was doubtless justified, since the rule of law must prevail, short-term bud-nipping methods cannot succeed so long as the British and the local governments remain apparently blind to any consideration of

African antifederation opinion. Mr. Franklin added that the development of non-co-operation and widespread passive resistance may be slow, if nothing worse, but if federation is bulldozed through, it will be certain. How right Mr. Franklin was can now be seen.

Central African Federation was conceived as a means of welding the Rhodesias and Nyasaland into an economic unit. The development of the Rhodesias as a federal unit is feasible as long as there is no excessive centralization of authority, for these territories are already heading toward a fair industrial-agricultural balance in their economies. But why drag in Nyasaland? Nyasaland has a permanent white population of only 500 (this excludes government officials and businessmen, who serve varying terms in the country and who, if added to the permanent settlers, would make a white population of about 5,000). The 2,500,000 Africans in this territory are for the most part cultivators; the economy of Nyasaland is agricultural, and black-white relations have hitherto been smooth and equable. But, according to the planners, Nyasaland, by far the smallest of the three territories, needs to develop her agricultural potential through partaking of the profits of industrial enterprise in the Rhodesias. In parentheses, reports of recent discoveries of rare minerals in Nyasaland are beginning to make many people wonder whether federation is economically necessary at all.

It is argued by those in favor of federation that it is the only possible way to materialize the proposed economic blueprint and that it is the only means of attracting the large capital investments which will have to be made for the exploitation of Central Africa's immense resources in uranium, gold, copper, lead, iron, hydroelectric power, coal, cotton, cattle, tobacco and cereals. They also see federation as a powerful stabilizing force. In its proponents' eyes federation can hold Africa to the free world, for Northern Rhodesia, Southern Rhodesia and Nyasaland as an economic unit are capable of inserting a wedge of freedom between the fascism of South Africa and the ugly, barbarous nationalisms typified by Mau Mau in Kenya.

The planners also express the fear that without a unifying organization the territories will fall piecemeal into the lap of South Africa. But why should this be? The Union has never pressed a claim to the control of these countries, nor have more than a handful of extremists in the Rhodesias suggested that the Union should do so. Relations between Britishers and Boers in South Africa have become so strained that rumors have been revived that Natal, which prides itself on being the most British state in the Union, is planning to secede. To judge from the temper of many people of British descent around Durban and Pietermaritzburg, both of which places I know quite well, I would say they were willing to do just that years ago, in some cases even before the nationalists assumed power. Rhodesians have the same attitude to the Boers as many of the residents of Natal. It seems most unlikely that British-dominated Northern and Southern Rhodesia, and an even more loyal Nyasaland, could ever be induced to become part of Boer-dominated

Africa, short, of course, of a physical struggle which is, again, more than unlikely. No, that argument will not do, since the settlers in the territories for which federation is proposed would have everything to lose and nothing to gain by joining the Union of South Africa at this or any other time.

Central Africa is ready for fuller industrial development; of that there is no doubt. But the decision to federate against the wishes of almost all the 6,000,000 inhabitants of the lands involved can only cause an unrest which will jeopardize the scheme from the beginning. The example of the Union of South Africa should have provided British authorities with a lesson on what can happen when an industrial revolution is carried through against a political background of unsolved racial discord: South Africa's experiments have produced not peace but a dangerous worsening of race relations. There is a powder trail from Pretoria to every town, village and hamlet in the Union of South Africa, and these trails may quickly spread to Central Africa now that federation is being imposed on Africans for "their own good," as the disciplinarians advise.

What of the natives' objections? To begin with, there are 6,000,000 natives compared with less than 200,000 Europeans in the Rhodesias and Nyasaland; in other words only three per cent of the total population is white. Yet the new constitution allots only six of the thirty-five seats in the federal assembly to Africans. And, if the scheme goes through as planned, no changes can be made in the allocation of seats for nine years, and only then if the proposed amendments are initiated by a two-thirds majority. Thus after nine years the white settlers could in theory make constitutional changes which would have a further adverse effect on the already underprivileged position of the Africans. As a safeguard against this happening we are told that the native leaders could apply to a board to be specially set up for forwarding to London any grievances they might have, but—and here is the rub—the African is not even given an assured majority on this board. Moreover, if London fails to heed present objections to federation, which the Africans are making known by all official and constitutional means open to them, how can they possibly be asked to rely on London's giving an ear to their future wishes?

Can it be so certain, after all, that federation will lead to such rapid social and economic progress? Why does political unification have to be necessary for this? There was already a wide measure of economic co-operation between the two Rhodesias, including a joint railway system and a customs agreement. There could be even more, irrespective of federation. The immense hydroelectric resources of the Zambezi River, which cuts between Northern and Southern Rhodesia, could be harnessed to the benefit of both territories, and railroads could be constructed to convey coal from the Wankie coal fields in Southern Rhodesia to the industrial areas in the north. Is federation necessary for the accomplishment of such programs? Can it lead to the production of even more copper? In view of the sullen opposition of native workers to the entire project it might easily be the

cause of a fall in production. How is the Southern Rhodesian color bar to be accommodated to the easier conditions prevalent in Nyasaland? Why did not the British
government postpone federation and instead invite the
three territories to put forward proposals for further
economic co-operation and give these a fair trial before
any attempt was made to force the scheme through?

Each side in this vital African question feels that its
political future is at stake. As elsewhere in Africa, the
whites see a threat to their privileged position in any increase of African responsibility. The Africans feel that
the whites are still their oppressors. Nor is it true, as
conservative elements have claimed, that the scheme is
everywhere supported by the moderates and opposed by
the extremists. The inarticulate masses are not taken into
account and virtually no Africans at all support the federation plan. Could it not be that the entire scheme is the
joint product of city-bred economists in London and
old-style imperialists in Africa, who in their anxiety to
maintain the outdated principle of white supremacy have
consciously turned their backs on dangers they must
know exist?

British opinions about Central African Federation are
sharply divided. The government's interpretation of the
referendum in Southern Rhodesia last spring as a mandate
to press on with federation aroused outspoken opposition
in Parliament, the press and in religious circles. The
Labor party opposed it not only because, being in opposition, it has a good opportunity to embarrass the government, but also because it is the heir of the Liberal

traditions of the last century. Mr. James Griffiths, the
former Labor government's foreign minister who is ac-
knowledged by the Conservatives themselves to be an
honest and competent student of African problems, made
an impassioned plea for much longer and deeper consideration when he broadcast to the British nation on
March 1, 1953. Mr. Griffiths stated that during his visits
to East, Central and West Africa he had felt the stirrings
of the same political consciousness which had already
transformed the face of Asia. In some places it is only
an undercurrent of discontent, he said, and confined to
grumbling against foreign rule. In others, like Nigeria
and the Gold Coast, it is already a well-developed de-
termination to achieve self-government. Some of its
forms are ugly, but whatever form it takes, it is a challenge, an opportunity and a choice. The only way forward lies in partnership, and the people of Britain, said
Mr. Griffiths, have the grave responsibility of guiding
the people of Africa toward a multiracial democracy.
Later on, when the fields of the Dark Continent are being
tilled and the wheels of the factories are turning, all the
world will benefit, but it will take a long, long time.
The European has a moral duty imposed on him by the
fact of the brotherhood of man. And Mr. Griffiths in
London and the white leaders in Central Africa all agree
that the white man's burden cannot yet be laid down.
The question is—which is the best way to carry it?

But Mr. Griffiths made this speech long before the
critical decisions of the summer of 1953. The Labor
opposition in London then proclaimed along with Mr.

Griffiths that if any step were to be taken which would accelerate the spread of racial strife in Central Africa, the disintegrating effects of such a situation would be felt throughout the entire continent. A short time ago Mr. Attlee stated, rather foolishly, I feel, that once the federation measure has been passed in London it will be the duty of all to try to make a success of the scheme.

I would like to quote comment from the London *Observer* since the point I wish to make is beautifully presented in its columns:

If this view [Attlee's] were accepted, it would leave the African opposition to the scheme without British friends and therefore more prone to the "Black Nationalist" attitude of which it is accused. For it would be absurd to expect the Africans of these territories to stop opposing the scheme because of what happens in Westminster where they are not only unrepresented and unheeded but refused the hearing they have requested.

Another influential voice, that of Doctor Geoffrey Fisher, Archbishop of Canterbury, urged grave deliberation. The conclusion to be drawn from African reactions, said Doctor Fisher, is not that the plan should be abandoned altogether, for that would be running away from the responsibilities of trusteeship for the native peoples, but that a much more detailed study be made of all segments of opinion. He reiterated that before federation is inaugurated there is an urgent need for imaginative action, promoted by trust and understanding, to demonstrate to Africans that the intention behind the federation scheme is to provide the necessary political and economic framework within which all races can move forward *in effective co-operation*. If these assurances cannot be given in Salisbury and Lusaka—the capital cities of Southern and Northern Rhodesia—as well as in London, then indeed the project should be dropped. Doctor Fisher has appealed not for constitutional safeguards alone, but for good will made effective in action, such as the removal of discriminatory legislation and some of the day-to-day practices which destroy racial harmony. The constitution for the federated states should, in Doctor Fisher's opinion, be reinforced by a bill of rights, setting out the claims which all federal citizens should have inviolably assured to them, whatever their race or voting power. The settlers of Central Africa have labored, and are laboring hard and well, to bring the benefits of prosperity and a promise for the future to these British lands. If they could now say with Abraham Lincoln, "As I would not be a slave, so I would not be a master," a new chapter in the British Commonwealth story could be begun.

Mr. Lyttelton, the present British Colonial Secretary, is a most fervent crusader in the cause of federation which, he declares, should have taken place three or even four years ago. The scheme, says Mr. Lyttelton, could give the Africans a chance to build an enduring home under the British conception of how races should live together. He claims that the European extremists, who believe in the policy of segregating the races and leaving the white man as the sole ruler of the country, would be encouraged by the failure of federation to pursue this idea; the African nationalists, believing that the control of Africa should be left exclusively to the Bantu peoples, would claim that they had diverted and deflected the white man from his purpose.

Headmen and chiefs who favor federation are afraid to come out in support of it, say the planners, and views prefabricated in England have been dumped on the Negro as if they were of African origin. In any case, they add, the difficulties of the subject are beyond the mental grasp of the great majority of Africans. It is true that the vocal native opposition to the scheme is coming from educated Africans who are the spokesmen of the African Congress. They may be few in number, but if they are so disposed, they are capable of spreading misinformation, which it is easier to do in a primitive and largely illiterate society. It may also be true that there has been some intimidation of chiefs who are favorably impressed by the federation plans. But the statement that the only African opposition is coming from a small band of extremists is dangerously misleading.

The Nyasaland chiefs who visited London in 1953 said on their departure from England in February that they were deeply disappointed at what they termed the "discourtesy" of the Colonial Secretary. Paramount Chief M'Bwera claimed that Mr. Lyttelton had been brusque and frowning and had lectured them instead of letting them put their case. He had insisted that there was *no public opinion* in Nyasaland and that ninety per cent of the natives did not know what federation was all about.

This the delegation denied most strenuously. After all, the fact that people may be unable to read and write does not mean that they are incapable of thinking and feeling. Nyasalanders feel very strongly that federation will lead to Southern Rhodesian domination, as it conceivably might, since Southern Rhodesia has more than three quarters of the total white population of the three territories. Another chief stated that Sir Godfrey Huggins, the Prime Minister of Southern Rhodesia, had been loud in his claims that federation could be a bulwark against the spread of Malanism. Africans do not see it like that: as far as most of them are concerned there is no difference between the native policies of Southern Rhodesia and South Africa, both of which they view with dread. Chief Maganga, a Moslem who fought in the British Army in two world wars, said he felt very strongly about the ethical aspects of the situation. Britain, said Chief Maganga, has a moral obligation toward Nyasaland which had *voluntarily* sought to be a British protectorate; and now Britain is proposing to sell Nyasaland to the white settlers of the Rhodesias.

These Nyasaland spokesmen poured scorn on the suggestion that the Central African Congress, from which most of the public opposition to federation is coming, is hostile to the loyal chiefs. The chiefs support Congress, they say, "because Congress is our child and faithfully represents African opinion." The party was sadly dismayed by the Colonial Secretary's refusal to let them have an audience with the Queen, their sovereign and protector. "What are we going to tell our people when we get home?" they asked in voices heavy with disillusionment.

African warnings are coming from all corners of all three lands. Federation will bring trouble, and, say the spokesmen, "it will not be of our seeking."

Resistance is solidifying. Representative chiefs from the Rhodesias and Nyasaland met at a central point, Fort Jameson in Northern Rhodesia, at the end of March 1953 to review the trend of events. The leader of the delegation from Southern Rhodesia, Joshua Nkomo, outlined the purpose of the gathering—the co-ordination of plans for "peaceful non-co-operation" if federation is established. Some Northern Rhodesian delegates were wearing badges provided, typically, by Indian traders, which bore pictures of Mahatma Gandhi with the inscription, "Gandhi, lover of peace." All indications so far show a desire for Gandhi's methods, but there are others on the side lines who are just waiting to promote incidents of the kind which precipitated the bloody scenes in Port Elizabeth in Cape Province not so very long ago. The more die-hard whites profess to believe that a passive resistance campaign will peter out after a short time. I think there is a greater probability that it would not be very long before extremists gained control of such a movement, for this will not be so difficult among Africans as it was among the Indians whose methods in India these extremists now propose to imitate.

The most tragic aspects of this whole ill-considered business are to be observed in Nyasaland. Though not overly prosperous, the Nyasas were progressive and loyal

subjects of the Crown. Since July 1953 they have organized a boycott of the coronation celebrations, refused
to volunteer for work in the mines and farms, failed to
pay their taxes, disobeyed forestry and veterinary regulations, turned their backs on meetings with government
officials and withheld supplies and porters. The Nyasaland chiefs are now working harmoniously with the
extremist Nyasaland African Congress.

Chief Mwase, who was chosen to attend the coronation but declined to go, is a man of the highest integrity
and intelligence. Until recently he counseled moderation
in the hope that some alternative to federation would be
put forward; by July 1953 he had abandoned hope and
wrote that war and everlasting hatred lay only a century
ahead. Chief Mwase was thinking in African terms of
time. The African nationalist leaders have no intention
of waiting more than a fraction of that time. There are
men in South Africa and the Rhodesias who are poised
ready to strike; in Kenya they have struck already.

Whichever view we take, the outlook in most parts of
Central Africa is gloomy. Even in the Congo where the
Belgians, busy as beavers, are building their economic
dams and in the French and Portuguese colonies where
the light of the industrial age has barely begun to dawn,
the African storm may be nearer than men think.

As for federation it seems to me that having allowed
the Africans in these territories to advance a few unsteady steps toward the light, the British government is
now turning around and placing the African in a position where it will be hard for him to achieve a redress

of any grievances he may have without resorting to un-
constitutional means. It was argued at the height of the
federation issue that British government withdrawal
could not be carried out without loss of face. But that
would have been nothing compared with the present
danger of the native question in the Rhodesias and Nyasaland becoming a mixture of the conditions prevalent in
Kenya and the Union of South Africa.

12

Tanganyika and Uganda

LONG BEFORE the British came, the Portuguese had combed every inlet of the East African coast from the Cape of Good Hope to Aden. The territory of Mozambique is still part of Portugal's African Empire, and farther to the north the influence of this intrepid seafaring people can still be seen and felt in spite of successive Arab occupations and present British rule.

In his voyage of 1497 Vasco da Gama rounded the Cape of Good Hope, sailed north to Mozambique, Mombasa and Malindi—in all of which places he reports finding Moslem traders—before cutting across to India. A century later the Portuguese occupied Zanzibar, then the most flourishing port on the entire coast. These events took place when Islam was declining as a military-religious organization, but the Portuguese explorers gained only a slippery foothold. The Europeans were later thrown out of Zanzibar by the Arabs during a new

Moslem ascendancy, and the virile empire of the Sultan Bargash ibn Said was stretched from Somaliland to Cape Delgado. Mombasa and Dar es Salaam, now the chief seaports of Kenya and Tanganyika, were once the strongholds of Arab traders whose dhows sailed from Aden and the ports of the Persian Gulf and back and forth to India. The riches of the hinterland of Zanzibar and Dar es Salaam raised the Hadhramaut and Arabia from decay.

But in the nineteenth century the Islamic dominions, once more riddled with corruption, failed to stand for long against vigorous newcomers from Northern Europe, and by 1880 the empires and sultanates had ceased to exist except in name. In 1890 Zanzibar, one of the most colorful towns in the world, became a British protectorate by an agreement under which Great Britain relinquished her claims on Madagascar in favor of France and ceded Heligoland to Germany. In accordance with the terms of an Anglo-German treaty of 1890 Great Britain acquiesced in the German occupation of Tanganyika—thus shattering Cecil Rhodes's dream of making Africa British from Cape Town to the Mediterranean.

Under German rule Tanganyika—German East Africa as it was officially called—was ruthlessly but efficiently developed. The southwestern part of the country was found to be especially suitable for European settlement: good livestock was raised, coffee, cotton and sisal hemp were introduced (the last-named has since become the colony's leading crop) and the mineral wealth of the country was exploited.

Then came the First World War. The campaign in

East Africa began with German attacks on the surrounding British territories and on the Belgian positions on Lake Tanganyika and Lake Kivu. The Allied blockade of Germany, however, prevented reinforcements reaching the embattled colony and the East African campaign degenerated into hit-and-run guerrilla warfare which ended in 1918 with the surrender of the German leader, General Paul von Lettow, who from all accounts had conducted his campaign with an almost medieval chivalry. The Allies made no allowances for this knightly attitude and the British, who accepted the mandate for Tanganyika in 1919, became responsible for a country whose transportation system and entire economic structure had been destroyed.

The postwar depression delayed the restoration of these essentials to the country's well-being and the early 1930s had been reached before the fortunes of Tanganyika began to revive. The Second World War passed Tanganyika by: there was no devastation of the countryside since there was no fighting in Central Africa, and the agricultural projects which were getting under way just prior to the outbreak of hostilities prospered under the stimulus of wartime's special needs.

Compared with Kenya, the Rhodesias, Nyasaland and the Union of South Africa, Tanganyika and Uganda are blessed lands, although with Central African Federation achieved, speculation has begun as to how long this happy situation will obtain. As yet, however, the problems of other territories come to the natives of Tanganyika and Uganda as far-off whispers. The peasantry goes about its increasingly prosperous business, unperturbed even by the closeness of the Mau Mau troubles. Tanganyika none the less experienced some uneasy stirrings which threatened trouble in the last months of 1951 and early in 1952. The British government spent a great deal of time just prior to 1950 in drawing up a comprehensive report on Tanganyika which included proposals for a new constitution. In 1950 the contents of a note prepared by Sir Edward Twining, the governor of Tanganyika, were allowed to leak out and were published in one of the East African newspapers. This memorandum, which set forth the possible directions constitutional reform might take, was later amid a general uproar officially dismissed as a trial balloon; in other words it was put out to test the reactions of the groups at which it was aimed.

The official report came out in August 1951, ostensibly to obtain the views of all races after the outcry over what will go down in local history as the "Tanganyika Cockshy." Several of the changes proposed in the report were very radical, and its reception was mixed. It will be well to remember that the document was prepared in the days of the Socialist government in Britain at a time when Fabian idealists were playing a large part in shaping colonial policy, and the Conservative legislatures of Kenya and Uganda as well as of Tanganyika felt it was aimed directly at them. In Kenya in particular there was an uproar in which some bitter words were directed at the authorities in London.

In short, what the reporting committee proposed was equal representation in an enlarged Legislative Council of all three of Tanganyika's main races—British, African and Indian. (As in the Union of South Africa many Indians entered Tanganyika as plantation workers.) In the new legislature it was proposed that there should be twenty-one members on the official body and a similar number on the unofficial (advisory) body—seven of each race in both groups. This was designed to supplant a Legislative Council of seven Europeans, four Africans and three Asians and an advisory committee of fifteen members, all nominated by the governor. The report went on to provide for elections, pointing out that an elected legislature would give the members more direct responsibility to the people.

As was only to be expected the European reaction was sharp and almost without exception unfavorable. The acting president of the Tanganyika European Council said that he considered that the only community which could stand to gain from such proposals was the Asian. The African certainly would not, he said, for equal representation at this stage would be a step detrimental to the African and his development.

The African leaders, whether or not they agreed with such a claim, kept quiet and showed wisdom and patience in urging their peoples not to create any disturbances. "We can best help the solution of our problems by refraining from making irresponsible and extreme demands," they said—a declaration which, I hope, will weigh heavily in the Tanganyika African's favor when future adjustments of colonial policy are made. The acting president of the council was right in his contention that the Asian group would be the one to gain; the Indians themselves apparently thought so too and supported the London proposals just as unanimously as the Europeans opposed them.

The views of the three races on the subject of the distribution of seats in the Legislative Council therefore seemed to be irreconcilable. This, said the *African World*, seems to have been the main reason for recommending equal representation, and it is regarded by many as a confession by the British authorities of weakness and inability to come to any conclusion on the ratio which would best serve the peoples and the development of the territory as a whole.

The Tanganyika uproar soon died down and today the country is smoothly and efficiently administered. There are evidences of an incipient racial partnership, the people are happy and the country moves contentedly from day to day. This tranquillity has not gone unnoticed by the Liberal elements in London, and the fact that the African in Tanganyika has a more adequate representation in the legislature than he does in some other African colonial territories is held up by many as proof that the racial partnership theory is not just so much vapor.

Against this it can be argued that the Tanganyika African, until 1919 a German serf, has not yet had time to catch up with the folk of the surrounding territories and is therefore not so articulate when it comes to expressing in terms of modern politics what he really feels. Even assuming that there is more than a grain of truth in this claim, the fact that a genuine effort is being made in the African's behalf in Tanganyika robs it of any serious propaganda value.

The problem of Indian representation in the Tanganyika legislature is more complicated. The Indian is still a rising financial power in the country. Many Indians are highly educated and are fully aware of the gravity of Africa's dilemma. But the Indian, like the European, comes from outside, and whether Hindu or Moslem his ties with India remain close. In view of the Indian's very understandable sympathy with the aims and ideals of the new India, this leads in many cases to a division of loyalties. As a Tanganyika legislator said recently, "I have a high regard for the Indian race. If they would only remember that they are Tanganyikans now and forget their Indian nationality, I would not care how many seats [in the legislature] they held."

The Swahili servants and bearers who entered Buganda with the white explorers corrupted the native name of the country to Uganda. A small African kingdom, Buganda, which is now part of the Uganda protectorate, is the only part of the country bearing the original name.

Sir John Hathorn Hall, governor of the territory until 1951, made a clear statement of policy regarding land tenure in Uganda, and if this is conscientiously followed—and the British are the most conscientious of administrators—it may be that the contrasting shadows of *apartheid* and native land hunger expressed in terrorism will never pass over this very British corner of Africa. For it has been clearly laid down that all Crown lands outside the trading centers in provinces other than Buganda, are being held in trust for the benefit of the African population. Secondly, although the right is reserved to the governor, as representing Her Majesty the Queen, to appropriate areas which he considers are required for forests, roads, townships or any other public undertakings, no steps will be taken until the African local governments have been consulted and full consideration given to their wishes. The government also undertakes not to alienate land to non-Africans except for agricultural and industrial undertakings which it is considered will promote the social and economic welfare of the inhabitants of the country, and for residential purposes only when a small area is involved. Nor is it intended that Uganda shall be developed as a country of non-African farming and settlement.

This is no new statement: it is in the nature of a reiteration of policy, since in the sixty years during which Uganda has been a British protectorate less than 500 square miles out of a total of over 80,000 have passed into non-African hands. Of this 500 square miles a mere 155 square miles of freehold and sixty-one square miles of leasehold land have been alienated by the Crown. The remaining 324 square miles represent purchases by non-Africans in Buganda before the passing of legislation in 1906 prohibited transfers without the written consent of the governor.

Naturally enough in the past there has been speculation as to the ultimate purpose of the government with regard to the Crown lands, and agitators have attempted to point to the continuing trusteeship as a British ruse covering designs for permanent possession. Mau Mau agents, who are known to have infiltrated into Uganda, have been working hard on this line of misrepresentation, but thus far there is no evidence to show that they are meeting with success except among the Uganda nationalists, who are a small minority. The proofs of good faith are strong and in the main the local governments are quite well satisfied with the arrangement under which rents from all leases of Crown land outside Buganda province are paid to the African authorities in whose areas such lands may be situated. In addition the protectorate government, while maintaining the mineral and forest rights, makes to the local governments an *ex gratia* payment, depending on the circumstances, of a portion of the royalties accruing from mining enterprises. Another welcome sign in these days of detribalization and the lumping of tribal identity into an amorphous mass is that district councils of the African local governments have been required to draw up bylaws concerning land tenure in accordance with tribal practice.

The years between 1860 and 1897 were a thirty-seven-year blood bath for the now peaceful protectorate of Uganda. The infamous 'Mtesa, a vicious despot of the M'siri school, profiting by the intense Christian-Moslem rivalry in the mission fields, let loose his hordes on the newcomers and all sorts of atrocities were committed.

'Mtesa's son Mwanga was, if anything, a more blood-

thirsty reprobate than his father and his continued perse-
cution of the whites—which included the murder in cold
blood of James Hannington, first Anglican bishop of
East Central Africa—only served to unite the Christians
and the Moslems as a temporary expedient. Mwanga
was dethroned, but during a fresh outbreak of missionary
strife he returned to power. His murderous regime continued, and the British government declared Uganda a
protectorate in 1894. Mwanga was allowed to remain in
the country on condition he behaved, but in 1897 further
trouble led to his banishment. But Mwanga was a durable
rogue: he was not yet finished, and when the Sudanese
troops which the British had brought to Uganda to maintain order rebelled, killing a number of whites, Mwanga
was not long in coming back to claim his throne. This
time, however, even his own people were not enthusiastic;
they had come to learn that Mwanga's visits brought
disaster in their train. So Mwanga, a fugitive, was hunted
down and sent under close arrest to the remote Seychelles
Islands in the Indian Ocean, where he died in 1903.

A country of fertile plateau, dense forests and equatorial swamps, everywhere tropical, wet and steamy from
the heavy rains, Uganda has put the Europeans to a severe
test. There have been ceaseless struggles with malaria,
sleeping sickness and venereal disease: the cutting and
maintenance of roads and railways have exhausted three
generations of empire builders. But for all that 7,500
Europeans and 36,000 Asians have settled there, and recent years have seen a remarkable improvement in living
conditions both for outsiders and Africans. Public-health

schemes and widespread general-hygiene propaganda are meeting with success, and increasing use is being made of mobile medical and dental units. One of my cousins, a dental surgeon, has one of these mobile dental wagons. He likes his work, but concedes that it will be many years before the roads are good enough to carry out drillings and extractions while the van is in motion!

Uganda is predominantly a country of peasant agriculture. Of its 80,000 square miles only 50,000 can be considered cultivable, and of this area only one fifth is under cultivation. The African family holding averages four acres; but if the native is to have a reasonable standard of living, a means must be found which will enable a family to work not four but at least twenty acres—and this would absorb all the land which is considered workable. But the development of the medical services and the consequent reduction in infant mortality have brought a rapid increase in the native population. It is estimated that the number of Africans will have doubled, that is to say will have reached 10,000,000, between twenty and thirty-five years from now. This complicates what on the face of it looks a matter of simple arithmetic, and since the area of the land cannot be doubled, its productivity must be increased. The already low standard of living will be lowered to danger point if methods of cultivation are not greatly improved, and then it is doubtful whether even with the most wholesale introduction of scientific methods production can be made to keep up with the rising birth and lowered mortality rates.

The emergency is being tackled realistically. It is

realized that the country must be developed industrially
in order to create an export business which will allow a
margin for the purchase of certain foodstuffs from
abroad. Meanwhile, the strides made in the agricultural
plan have created prosperity in peasant circles. The
knowledge that this prosperity may be temporary has
caused a speeding up in the industrial program, and the
establishment of heavy and secondary industries is being
stimulated by every possible means.

It is indeed fortunate that Uganda has the raw materials, both mineral and vegetable, to feed such enterprises. The country's lack of coal is offset by the great
hydroelectric project at Owen Falls on the Nile between
Lake Victoria and the Murchison Falls. The governor
of Uganda stated in 1952 that at this point the potential
of electrical energy is as great as the entire production by
all methods in Great Britain today. A glance at the already known mineral deposits shows the possibilities for
industrial development. Cobalt and copper exist in large
quantities at Kilembe, at the foot of Ruwenzori near the
Belgian Congo border. At Kigezi there are wolfram, tin
and bismuth. Lead is being extensively mined to the east
of Lake George, and there are sizable deposits of uranium,
though in low concentration, on the eastern frontier. At
Tororo, almost on the Kenya line, there are what are
probably the largest phosphate concentrations in the
world, and with these are mixed magnetite iron and
vermiculite, a substance which is being increasingly used
in insulation compounds. There is a complex mineral
field at Sukulu, where within a radius of only two and a

half miles are to be found phosphates, limestone, iron, zirconium and pyrochlore, a species of niobium, which is a component of the heavier heat-resisting alloys used in the manufacture of jet engines.

The plan for the exploitation of these resources, which includes the installation of factories for the processing of ores and the manufacture of consumer goods, has many features in common with the Belgian Ten-Year Plan for the development of the Congo. The niobium at Sukulu alone has been estimated by a series of drillings to be worth nearly $300,000,000. Copper and cobalt could be produced in quantities to compete with the Belgian Congo and at less cost in labor, for the Congo is working under the handicap of inflationary prices which do not prevail in the British colonies. There is already an effective demand in East Africa itself for 100,000 tons of superphosphates.

Assurances have been given to the native chiefs and notables who were rather afraid at the inception of this industrial plan that large portions of their land would be alienated. The British government has reaffirmed that all possible land will be preserved for the farmer, and that used-out mine workings will, where possible, be reclaimed for agricultural use. In any case mines, factories and workshops take up only a fraction of the surface area of the most highly industrialized countries. And these factories can provide not only a means of livelihood for many thousands of Africans, but also, given the will to succeed, native workers can rise in time to positions of higher responsibility on both the technical and the executive levels. This is no pipe dream, for a common-sense land policy has done much to forestall the industrial unrest which would almost certainly have supervened if industrialization had been forced on an uprooted and land-hungry peasantry.

Uganda has possibilities for becoming the showcase of British Africa. In spite of the difficulties under which agricultural projects are being pushed forward, this country is already producing more cotton and cotton seed and more coffee than any other British colony in Africa. It produces more peanuts—a valuable oil producer—than any colony other than Nigeria. By far the greater part of the locally grown tobacco used in the manufacture of cigarettes and pipe tobacco in East Africa comes from Uganda. This territory has an exportable surplus of maize and sugar and a variety of other food and cash crops. Indeed it is a remarkably productive little country when all its impediments are taken into consideration.

What Sir Winston Churchill said a long time ago, back in 1907, holds today. "Uganda," he said, "is alive. It is vital and in my view it ought in the course of time to become one of the most prosperous of all our East and Central African possessions. My counsel plainly is: 'Concentrate upon Uganda.' Nowhere will the results be more brilliant, more substantial, or more rapidly realized." These are the words of a great prophet: it has taken a long time and two world wars to realize their truth. And now, at last, we are maybe beginning to see the fruits of honest statesmanship, for Uganda is one of the few candles burning in a dark African world.

Yet there is a latent threat. Though it is to be hoped that the British government will leave well alone politically, the British Colonial Secretary, Mr. Lyttleton, who remained deaf to all African protests over Central African Federation, has made no secret of the fact that he dreams of meddling not only in Uganda, but in Kenya and Tanganyika as well. We must marvel at this man's singleness of purpose and pray that time or a change of government in London will bring in a more liberal "official" conception of Britain's African responsibilities. In a speech to the East African Club in London in July 1953, Mr. Lyttelton said that at some future date Uganda, Kenya and Tanganyika might be better off under an East African Federation.

Reaction in Uganda was sharp and unequivocal. African, Asian and the white settlers unhesitatingly condemned the suggestion, and relations between the Colonial Office in London and the local populations rapidly became cool. The speech was all the more ill-considered in that it provided the African extremists, who are trying to hold the Uganda National Congress together, with some first-class propaganda material.

What hit hardest among all sections of the population was the hint of political federation with Kenya. Central African Federation has brought the Africans of the Rhodesias and Nyasaland to the verge of rebellion. A number of settlers' leaders in Kenya are advocating a tie-up between Kenya and the new Federation as a preliminary to the political unification of all six British territories. Since Kenya is viewed with suspicion by both Uganda and Tanganyika, strong opposition to any sort of federation is being voiced in both countries. The fact that Mr. Lyttelton implied that his dream could not become reality in the near future does not detract from the untimeliness of his utterance. Last July Mr. Colin Legum, an African expert whom no one can accuse of being overly radical, wrote from Entebbe, the capital of Uganda:

Uganda, like the Gold Coast, has a strong peasant agriculture which is enjoying great economic prosperity. Traditional colonial policy has been to develop Uganda as an independent African state—a development which would be sharply retarded by any question of political federation.

Official and unofficial observers here are deeply puzzled over what prompted Mr. Lyttelton to make a statement which is hopelessly out of tune with local sentiments, policies and aspirations.

13

Kenya

KENYA IS THE most "colonial" of Britain's colonies. The settlers, a fair proportion of whom are well-to-do farmers with aristocratic connections back home or retired senior officers of the British services, still refer to their home as "Kenya Colony."

There has been a tendency both in Britain and abroad to regard Kenya largely as a land of remittance men, moneyed wastrels and blimps. Nothing could be farther from the truth. The Kenya farmer is a shrewd operator, and the standard of farming, considering the unreliability of much of the available labor, is very high. But until the recent troubles, Kenya landowners all too frequently set themselves apart from and 'way above the civil servants and businessmen of Nairobi and Mombasa and regarded the whites of Uganda, Tanganyika and Nyasaland with superior scorn. This was brought home to me in a cocktail-party squabble between a lady, whose husband was a business executive, and a retired regular officer who was somewhat pinker than his gins. The exchanges ended with the lady dismissing the ex-soldier and his maudlin jingoisms with "Oh, he's just another Kenya Stiff." Retorted the gentleman: "That, madam, coming from a merchant's wife, I take for what it is worth." Exaggerated? Not on your life. That sort of attitude was unfortunately all too common before Mau Mau became the password which brought all white men together.

As for Rhodesians—the men of Kenya lumped them with the despised South Africans. If you lived south of Lusaka, you were a "Yahpi," in other words, a Boer. Recently there has been a softening in the attitude of the farmer-soldiers toward the townsmen of Kenya, but in the main they continue to show the same lack of respect for outsiders, particularly visiting delegations from London and colonists from the other territories, as they always did.

For all their faults these men have been conscientious and responsible in training their native help. It is not to be wondered at that the relationship between the two is rather like the historic one of prince and peasant, for, seeing England "going to the dogs" and resenting the rise in wealth and social status of the merchant class, many of them came out to Africa to re-create the conservative England of the fox-hunting squires. These are the men whose refusal to face facts until the last few years and who by their dismissal of manifestations of native unrest as just another bunch of "Kukes (Kikuyu) getting out of hand" have allowed native discontent to reach its present alarming proportions. As for communist penetration, nothing to their minds could be more absurd.

Yet in facing the situation as it is evolving at present, these Kenya landowners and farmers are showing the finest qualities of leadership; they have organized themselves, their hereditary skill as soldiers and campaigners is being displayed at its best and, in the tradition of Waterloo, they are keeping calm.

The trouble in Kenya might have been avoided if the British Colonial Office had had a more clear-cut plan in the first place. The administrator and the civil servant were at too great a distance both physically and mentally from the farmer to prevent unscrupulous elements' getting in and exploiting both farmer and native. The early settlers were not businessmen. They were pioneers working virgin soil and had to look around for outlets for their produce. They were swindled by merchants whom they distrusted previously and have despised since, while their workers, with typical African improvidence, soon found themselves in the clutches of Indian and Arab moneylenders and traders. These experiences caused large numbers of the colonists to set themselves apart and dream out their Kiplingesque dream. Appropriating much of the best farming land, they withdrew into themselves, paying little heed to the deteriorating conditions their action was causing among the rapidly increasing native population. The awakening has been rude.

It is a tragedy that the ugly manifestations of native

unrest had to strike such a beautiful country. The highlands around Nairobi, though they straddle the equator, have a temperate, almost European, climate. European crops can be grown alongside coffee, cotton, maize and sisal. Cattle thrive and the land abounds in big game. And the Europeans, in possession of the best land, do not intend to be dispossessed. In any case, they say, if the native were to inherit the land he would ruin it in a generation or even less.

Maybe they would have had a point there some years ago, but the progress of the African farmer in recent years seriously weakens this argument when it is used nowadays. Maybe the native when left to himself *is* an indolent and wasteful cultivator, but he is *not* being left to himself. He is being instructed and helped: such incentives as guaranteed prices for his produce have shown him how labor is applied economics. A spark of pride in achievement has been created. But it would not be natural to expect that the firmly entrenched Europeans would look favorably on any suggestions that they should sell out to make way for native settlement of these rich areas, nor has any official body been so foolish as to hint that they might. Furthermore, being what they are, Mau Mau terrorism has only served to stiffen their attitude.

As was to be expected, the "Tanganyika Cockshy" caused no little stir in Kenya, the proposed increase in Asian representation in the legislature being particularly disturbing to Kenya Europeans. These men and women are not the sort who stand aside and make no protest. A

meeting of the Kenya Electors' Union applauded the
views of a speaker who declared that if the proposed new
constitution for Tanganyika were an attempt to set the
pattern for Kenya, *such an attempt would fail.* The same
speaker went on to say that the Kenya Electors had a
right to intervene in Tanganyika and that Sir Godfrey
Huggins and Sir Roy Welensky in Southern and Northern Rhodesia took the same view. Consciously or un-
consciously this spokesman was aligning the Kenya Europeans with the chief proponents of the Central African
Federation scheme which is so bitterly opposed by nearly
all the Bantu peoples. He even used the same arguments
up to a point:

Whatever may be the ideals of the political theorists
in the United Kingdom, there remains the basic fact that
from Cape Town to Nairobi there are European leaders
and backward natives in juxtaposition. It is useless to
suppose that the problem could be solved in one place by
one method and in another place by a different method.

In this particular speech the Indian population was not
mentioned, but the Indian attitude is noteworthy. The
Indian is very thick-skinned. For years he has been
swallowing insults and accumulating money, and his ability to do both with equanimity has made him a widely
mistrusted being. Loan oft loses both itself and friend;
thus the Indian, frequently intimidated when he threat-
ens to sue, is the holder of a host of bad debts, African
and European alike.

It is not so very long since the first Indian workers

came to Kenya. They quickly summed up the weaknesses of the Bantu, and in no time disreputable-looking little Indian general stores were springing up all over the countryside. Never spending a penny themselves, living on a handful of rice a day and sleeping at night under the counter of their one-room stores, they grew rich if not fat. Their children and grandchildren are both—so much so that when the Aga Khan, spiritual leader of the Moslems among them, made one of his visitations to East Africa some years ago he was presented with the equivalent of his weight in diamonds. The sons and grandsons of the Indian trader are entering the learned professions: they show considerable aptitude as doctors and lawyers. They are likable, intelligent, highly respected in their own communities and tolerated by the liberal-minded white "fringe."

Yet there is good reason for thinking that the Indian is meddlesome, that he is fundamentally anti-British and that he is using the native as a cat's-paw. It is no secret that India would be only too happy to unload some of her surplus population in East Africa. An Indian Deputy Minister for Foreign Affairs stated publicly that East Africa is climatically and geographically the most suitable sphere for Indian immigration, adding that he would like to see the doors of East Africa open to Indians for he felt they could play a large part in the development of the country. He even went on to say that he would like to see 100,000 Indians emigrate to East Africa. The British government, said the Indian spokesman, had relayed this statement to the East Africa legislatures. "The results,"

he concluded rather plaintively, "were most disappointing." So disappointing were they in fact that the Com-
missioner for Indian Affairs in East Africa felt compelled
to make a face-saving claim that India is not seeking an
outlet for her surplus population in East Africa or elsewhere.

As for native "cat's-paws," the smoldering Indian resentment against the European ruling class has led him
to turn his talents to political intrigue, an occupation for
which nature has fitted him perfectly. In 1951 the Kenya
Weekly News said outright, and no denial was forthcoming, that the Africans, advised and encouraged by
certain Hindu politicians, were pressing for ten seats in
the Kenya Legislative Council and two seats in the Executive Council.

The native leaders of Kenya were quick to perceive
that the whites did not all see eye to eye with one another
and for many years subversive movements have been at
work in the country. A genuine land hunger among
Kenya's peasantry has been encouraged by the half-
informed and exploited by the evilly disposed.

Mau Mau, which is the latest in the series of expres-
sions of native unrest, is more serious than its predeces-
sors in that it is organized and directed by shrewd brains.
Mau Mau is a secret society; its membership is confined to
the Kikuyu people. Yet the Kikuyu are intelligent and
industrious. The most politically and socially conscious
of the native races of Kenya, they are recognized as the
group most likely to prove their worth when entrusted
with a certain measure of self-government. How then

can Mau Mau's lapse into voodoo, witchcraft and savagery be explained? There is a genuine social and
economic background to these disorders of which Communist agitators are taking full advantage, but only a
small proportion of the initiates of Mau Mau are fully
conscious of it. On the other hand there exists in very
definite measure an organized assault on the established
order by the die-hards of witchcraft. The exact extent
of the interplay will never be determined.

One thing is sure: Mau Mau's aims, if not always its
methods, are viewed sympathetically by the educated
detribalized African. In the banks, offices, schools, laboratories and medical centers of Africa's new cities are to
be found black men with European educations and, superficially at any rate, European outlooks. And here to
a large measure are to be found the agitators who harness
the forces of witchcraft to their schemes.

These men are not always entirely to blame. I have
had some experience with the way the colored student
can be treated in England, for example. These men and
women, newly arrived in London or at one of the large
provincial university cities, are lonely. Though England
professes no color bar, colored folk are so few and such
a rarity that British townsmen, aside from Londoners,
either are shy of them or ignore them completely, while
rustics regard them with openmouthed and unconstruc-
tive curiosity. Thus, though there is no positive ill
feeling toward the African visitors on the part of their
British hosts, there is little organized entertainment to
take care of the black students' leisure hours. I am not

belittling the efforts of the Y.M.C.A. and the churches, but they do not advertise themselves sufficiently and the visitors all too often are left alone to become easy prey for Communist-front groups who, under the cloak of liberalism, turn them into embittered souls. Jomo Kenyatta, the prime mover of Mau Mau who is now serving a seven-year prison sentence, is a good example. He has lived and studied in England, has an English wife and a son. His leftist tendencies have been exploited; he visited Moscow as a "guest" and finally deserted his wife and child. A few years ago he reappeared as the director of a proscribed native "welfare" organization which was undoubtedly a front for Mau Mau and undercover Communist activities.

Mau Mau is nothing new; the poison has been at work for years. It is a symptom and not the disease itself. If we look at the precursors of Mau Mau we can see a similar pattern in which a cunning use has been made of modern formulas to perpetuate and even justify witchcraft in the eyes of the more backward natives, at the same time blinding them to the real aims of the leaders.

Some three years ago a district officer, two European police officers and a native tribal policeman were speared to death by tribesmen at a place called Kolloa, near Lake Baringo, in Kenya. Twenty-nine of the attackers were killed by rifle fire. Just before this, in the district court of Kiambu, the district officer had been investigating charges of the unlawful administration of an oath brought against a large number of Africans. One of the specific charges was that a Kikuyu had administered an oath to a fellow Kikuyu binding him to obey the orders and commands of a society which had been declared prejudicial to public security in the colony.

The Crown witness described how he was given two pieces of goat's meat and told to bite and swallow a piece of each one seven times. Other pieces were then passed round his head and legs seven times, after which the initiator dipped a twig into the animal's entrails and placed the end against the new member's mouth. This was also done seven times. The witness was then told that if he mentioned this to anyone he would die. Finally the sign of the cross was made on his forehead in blood while he repeated after his mentor, "May the British Empire kneel as we are kneeling."

This Lake Baringo affair grew out of the fanatical teachings of a cult which was based on a distorted interpretation of the Bible. The damage goes back to the time when the simplest Biblical teaching was apt to be harnessed to heathen cults: throw a dose of politics into the mixture and we have affairs like this and similar ones.

In East Africa this xenophobia has been evident in the activities of four main sects, of which the *Dini ya Msamba*—the Religion of the Old Customs—has the worst record. This group was responsible for the Baringo murders and for an earlier riot at Malikisi in 1948 when the police were forced to fire and the sect lost eleven killed. The *Watu ya Roho*—the Holy Rollers—had a reputation for incendiarism; the leader of the *Ndi ya Jesu Kristo* was hanged for his part in what became known as the Gatundu murders of 1947, when a police officer was hacked to death by a frenzied mob. The lesser-known, but not less subversive *Watu ya Mungu*—Men of God— is an offshoot of the Holy Rollers.

In August 1950 the *African World* warned that apart from these illegal pseudoreligious sects, the activities of an entirely political group of natives with nationalist aspirations were increasing. Here for the first time I saw Mau Mau mentioned without being named.

The Kikuyu Central Association, by means of secret meetings and a considerable underground organisation, has succeeded in persuading Kikuyu to take an oath on the following lines: "We will not reveal anything to Government, and we will give Government no assistance: we will not allow any part of the Kikuyu land unit to be taken away and we will refuse to sell land to a European."

There was in fact never any question of Kikuyu land being taken away.

However bad the situation may be from the native's point of view, Mau Mau, which seeks to redress grievances by terrorism, can never provide a satisfactory solution. Over 3,000 British troops were quickly dispatched to Kenya at the beginning of the insurrection and the arrival of two additional infantry battalions together with corps and supply troops in mid-1953 raised the strength of the garrison to 6,000. The settlers themselves formed commandos (a word borrowed, ironically enough, from the Boers), loyal Kikuyu were armed and the retaliation was sharp and effective. Mau Mau murder suspects were shot, or hanged from portable gallows; thousands of Kikuyu were taken from the cities and the farms and sent back to native reserves where they faced starvation in a land destroyed by erosion and many years of their own mismanagement.

The appointment of General Sir George Erskine in May 1953 to conduct the campaign against the terrorists showed that the British government was committed to a policy of hitting first and asking questions afterward. General Erskine, whose firm and capable handling of the situation in the Suez Canal zone in 1952 made him an ideal choice for the Kenya emergency, quickly mounted a campaign which turned the murderers into fugitives. This change in the fortunes of Mau Mau encouraged the leaders of the loyal Kikuyu in their resistance to the terrorists. Emboldened by government successes, prominent Kikuyu leaders declared that extermination was the only means of dealing with the dreaded secret society.

When the emergency was declared in Kenya in the fall of 1952, it was revealed that some seventy per cent of the Kikuyu people had taken the Kikuyu oath for one reason or another; in some areas the proportion was as high as ninety-five per cent. At that time Mau Mau had the upper hand and the vast majority were terrorized and intimidated into aligning themselves with the movement. Now the picture is very different and the Kikuyu people are divided by civil war. But Mau Mau, though it may be suppressed, will never be obliterated by the methods now being used, and by August 1953 many people were beginning to realize this. A great deal of support was given to suggestions that Kenyatta and his colleagues

should be released and asked to tour the country telling
the people to observe peace. A member of the Kenya
Legislative Council, Colonel Ewart Grogan, prepared a
statement for publication in which, referring to the Kenyatta proceedings, he said:

Africans are bewildered and Europeans exasperated at
the whole legal approach. Perpetuation of this process
will surely be deemed by the outside world as persecu-
tion. The moment would seem right for a bold and generous move on a psychological plane by invoking the
assistance of probably disillusioned men in preventing a
complete disruption of a normally friendly and progressive tribe.

The timing of the Mau Mau outbreak, coming as it did
when a good proportion of the Kenya Europeans were
still distrustful of Whitehall's colonial policy, showed
that a far-flung intelligence system had been at work for
some time. The sentencing of Kenyatta and his associates
at a time almost coincident with the Southern Rhodesian
referendum and the South African elections may turn out
to have been a blunder of the first magnitude, for all comment which has reached me since has indicated that these
three events have led to a noticeable hardening of anti-
white opinion in the colonial territories.

For Kenyatta, irrespective of whether or not he is a
Communist, is looked on as a symbol of African liberation and progress throughout the entire continent. Many
natives who regard the Mau Mau outrages with loathing
nevertheless have a great deal of admiration for Ken-

yatta's educational and political achievements. Before sentence was passed on Kenyatta and before the momentous South African election and the Southern Rhodesian referendum, a protesting voice was raised in South Africa by the influential liberal newspaper of Manilal Gandhi.

If Kenyatta is thrown into prison, if Southern Rhodesia votes for federation, and if Malan is returned to power in South Africa, an altogether new situation will arise in Africa. *The peoples of Africa will have cause seriously to consider a joint continental solution.*

It needs little imagination to see what that solution would be, in spite of all the talk about passive resistance. Walter Sisulu, secretary of the African Congress, commented:

Kenyatta is no racialist. We Africans resent Britain's method of suppressing the people by force of arms instead of negotiating with their leaders. This method makes the entire African people bitter against the British government. We regard Mau Mau as a legitimate organization of the Kenya Africans.

And the leader of the South African Indian Congress had his say: "Seemingly the judgment [against Kenyatta] is political and comes from a despotic administration."

Most of the Kenya Europeans are Conservative to the marrow in matters of politics. They welcomed the return of their party to power at the last general election, but they have not forgotten the visit of Mr. James Grif-

fiths to Kenya and are afraid that British colonial policy
may have been modified beyond possibility of change
during the years of Labor administration. The Socialists
gave the African more reason to hope for a share in the
government of his country than any other administration
had done, and the African Europeans saw in every Socialist move in the colonial field an insidious and determined attempt to weaken the position of the white
settlers and increase the legislative power of other races.
They had good grounds for their beliefs, for in April
1951 it was reported that the governor of Kenya had told
a delegation of representatives of the Kenya African
Union that he was prepared to propose that there should
be more Africans on the Kenya Legislative Council than
hitherto. Mr. Griffiths' statement, "The election of an
African Parliament on the Gold Coast is one stage—others
will follow," seemed to provide a justification for European fears.

At the time of the fall of the Labor government the
African had his foot in the government door. With agitators working very cleverly to nullify any conciliatory
moves the British authorities might make, African discontent has culminated in Mau Mau.

Yet despite the turmoil in Kenya, the authorities are
going ahead with their schemes for improving African
living conditions. These are very bad indeed in the cities,
where the native quarters are custom-built breeding
grounds for sedition. For example Pumwami, an African
suburb of Nairobi, a squalid huddle of mud huts with
corrugated-iron roofs, is riddled with underground Mau

Mau activity. The wretched hovels of Pumwami are owned mostly by local Arabs, a harsh usurious set who command exorbitant rents. The aspiring African youth, disgusted with his economic conditions and looking with envious eyes at the European way of life, is an easy target for the blandishments of Mau Mau and the Communist alike. I fear it is too late for housing improvements to have the significance they might have had if calm had prevailed, or even been restored promptly after the first Mau Mau outrages. But as experiments in financed housing they are worth noting. Building plots which are all for residential use are offered to Africans who wish to build or rent houses constructed in accordance with approved plans and in permanent materials. A lot sixty feet by thirty feet can be obtained for 100 shillings (fourteen dollars) for a lease of twenty years with the option of renewal for a further twenty-five years unless the lot is required for town-planning purposes. There is to be no rent for the first five years and a nominal rent of seventy cents a month thereafter. Loans in the form of materials are made to those Africans who wish to build their own homes, and cash loans are available for those who wish to buy ready-built homes. This scheme is honestly and generously inspired, but it does little more than scratch the surface of the problem.

If the present unhappy situation could be put aside, we could see that farming in Kenya is an attractive and usually profitable occupation for Europeans. There is more machinery nowadays, although buying machinery for use by native labor can still be a hazard in spite of continued improvement on the native's part. And the European must show more willingness to run the machinery himself than he has done previously. The capital outlay is high. Cleland Scott, an expert on East African development, estimates that to set up as a farmer in Kenya requires some $25,000 in addition to a loan from the Land Bank. Suitable land is available but by no means plentiful and, owing to increasing settlement, prices are high. A small mixed farm of, say, 500 acres needs plenty of rainfall, which automatically restricts the choice to certain areas: boreholes and dams eat large holes in capital resources. However, a mixed farmer has a wide choice—wheat, oats, barley, maize, sunflower and linseed. If the farm is high enough, pyrethrum, a small mountain daisy, is a sure dollar earner, but this can be considered only if the land is over 7,000 feet above sea level. In Kenya today any farmer can apply for what is called the Minimum Guaranteed Return: this means that as soon as his crops are planted he can obtain a predetermined price per acre. This price used to be about ten dollars, but has probably risen in the last year or so.

"Daisy farmers" have a crop which yields an insecticide, pyrethrin, which still holds its own against any number of synthetic rivals. What is needed is altitude—the best crops grow at levels between 8,500 and 9,000 feet—and a plentiful supply of native help. Pyrethrum is essentially a "plantation crop." It grows in almost any kind of soil provided it is not waterlogged, and its powder can easily be dried out in the sun. Concerning farming in Kenya in general Scott says: "Provided you are not too proud to sit on a tractor yourself, and to use your hands, you will get by—and at least you will be working in an equable climate with plenty of sunshine."

These sunny words are ringed by black clouds: at the moment the plowshares of Kenya stand to be beaten back into guns. Jomo Kenyatta in prison is a challenge to his countrymen; there are others to take his place and conduct the terrorist campaign. For fear lest Mau Mau should gain a foothold among hitherto co-operative tribes such as the Luo, the Bahluya and the Kipsigi, the governor of Kenya ordered the arrest of the Luo leader Fanuel Odede, who took over the presidency of the Kenya African Union after Kenyatta was apprehended. But even assuming Mau Mau terrorism fails, we shall need a fresh approach to Kenya's grave problems; and if peace is to be maintained, I cannot see any solution which will not entail some measure of compromise with, or even of eventual capitulation to, the growing African claims for self-determination. The battle for the minds of Africans and for their participation in a multiracial African society has, as yet, hardly begun.

14

French Equatorial Africa

FRENCH EQUATORIAL AFRICA, known until 1910 as the French Congo and still referred to as such by the Old Africa Hands, is really a group of four French colonial possessions. Bounded on the north by the French Sudan, on the west by the Atlantic Ocean, on the southwest by the Belgian Congo, and on the northeast by the Anglo-Egyptian Sudan, French Equatorial Africa covers about 1,000,000 square miles, which is roughly the size of its neighbor, the Belgian Congo.

The four colonial territories, Gabon, Middle Congo, Ubangi-Shari and Chad, are each administered by a lieutenant governor under the supreme command of the governor-general, whose headquarters are at Brazzaville. There was a time when Brazzaville was known as Poto-Poto. That was at the turn of the century, and apart from the name little has changed there since the days when Savorgnan de Brazza, Stanley's French rival, laid claim to the north bank of the Congo River in the name of the French Republic.

When I wanted to try to capture something of the spirit of Africa's colonial past, it was an easy matter for me to take a ferry across the oily steel-colored swell of the Congo. A distance of four miles and a lapse of twenty minutes is all that separates Leopoldville—bustling, modern and Belgian—from sleepy, old-colonial, French Brazzaville.

It used to make me feel like an adventurer to step off the neat Belgian ferryboat, cross a derelict railroad, pass the run-down Hôtel du Beach and stride quickly along a lane flanked with bungalows which are now little better than hovels, the achievement of some pioneer realtor who has long since passed on. At the crossroads as I turned left there used to be—and surely still is, if he is alive—a native tailor with a hand-operated Singer sewing machine. There he would sit, surrounded by bales of gaudy cloth, under an awning draped with the abandoned webs of generations of spiders.

Around the corner there opened out a vista of quaint French-colonial streets, rotting vegetation, slovenly, sun-blackened, bearded Frenchmen, little yellow dogs and ever-open bars. There is an air of decay about Brazza-ville which the all-pervading stench of French brandy cannot freshen. Its taxis are broken-down Citröens and French Fords, its roads are studded with potholes the size of moon craters; the ornate shutters of its public buildings hang on one hinge and need several coats of paint.

But Brazzaville has a French soul. Here, where exiles

and time-serving French civil servants and soldiery dream
of the Place Pigalle and the Champs Élysées, the cooking
and the wines are French; garlic rides the air and co-
quettish laughter rings in smoky cafés filled with equatorial blondes and unshaven men. I loved Brazzaville
from the first time I was there. After the humorless nose-
to-the-grindstone commercialism of Leopoldville, this
transported Paris slum was a place where I could relax
and dream, where I could eat roast lamb so spiced with
garlic it could have been smelled six tables away if the
occupant of every other table in the room had not also
been sitting in a miasma of garlic which made him
shimmer like a mirage. A call for water was greeted by
the waiters with a shrug and a polite sneer: wine or nothing was the rule. And afterward a glass of fifty-year-old
cognac would appear at my elbow along with the pear-
shaped proprietor, and we would discuss the shortcom-
ings of unadventurous British and American cooking
while trying to modify the taste of the garlic with the
strongest of French *caporal* cigarettes.

In 1950 and 1951 Brazzaville had something of a boom.
Some of the vast amounts of capital brought out from
troubled Indochina by nervous French investors began
to find their way to this last outpost of the French Empire.
But this ephemeral prosperity made very little difference
to the everyday life of the Brazzaville *poilu*—the unshaven
one. The dazzling white buildings, the expensive new
restaurants and the influx of new cars went unnoticed by
him. Poto-Poto International Airport with its flashy, almost surrealist reception and departure halls and its

chromium-plated cocktail lounge merely drew forth his scorn. Unchanging and unchangeable, one day a mechanic, the next a pastry cook, the Old Africa Hand wastes hours of political and philosophical discourse on the steaming air and achieves nothing. On Bastille Day, French Independence Day, he helps put on a show. The champagne and the Pernod flow and the bands play, but behind the gaiety, the wit and the sparkle it is not difficult to sense that same disillusionment and cynicism which every Frenchman one meets these days tries so courageously, yet unavailingly, to hide.

I said good-by to Brazzaville a year ago. The energy of the past two years seemed to be grinding slowly to a halt. The antlike workers of a month before were again draped listlessly over their café tables. Yes, things were back to normal, and my last impressions as I set foot on the steamy quayside were of a smell of overripe bananas and a weary French customs official, with *képi* askew and tunic unbuttoned, appearing sheepishly from the darkness of his shed and asking us with wine-laden breath, *"Rien à declarer?"*

Lest any of you should think that I love to wallow in squalor, let me hasten to assure you that this is not so. It is merely that squalor becomes tolerable after the excessive neatness and the carbolic soap-scented commercial piety of Brazzaville's very unidentical twin, Leopoldville. I have been a Francophile ever since I can remember, and I found it heartbreaking to see how the misfortunes of the motherland show through the threadbare gaiety of

the cities of France's African Empire. The garbage-
littered, run-down streets of Brazzaville, Pointe-Noire,
Libreville and Douala quickly narrow into jungle trails
beyond the city limits: the lanes peter out, hiding their
heads in thickets, weeds and sand dunes as if not daring
to point the way across the wildernesses which spread
northward to the line where stunted bush gives way to
the limitless Sahara.

In this neglected land is Lambaréné, the home of the
Nobel prize winner Albert Schweitzer. Missionary, doctor, organ designer and perhaps the world's greatest authority on the interpretation of Bach, this man of genius
has cut himself off from the fleshpots and lives among his
beloved Africans in a remote corner of Equatorial Africa.
Doctor Schweitzer seems hardly conscious of the homage
paid him by the world. He is concerned only with his
healing and civilizing mission: even his music has to be
set aside when suffering humanity needs him. I have
never been to Lambaréné, although nowadays it can easily be reached by air. To my shame, I, like the majority
of whites in Central Africa, have tended to take for
granted the presence of a scholar and saint in our midst.
In this book I cannot do more than pay him passing homage, though he has been in my mind a great deal of the
time as I have been writing. If every European in Africa
were a Schweitzer, or even partly one, there would be no
African storm to fear.

Lambaréné is a tiny place, lying like a small island in a
vast sea of bush. How many natives receive physical and

spiritual benefit from it would be hard to estimate. Yet it is a value, a civilizing spiritual value in the wilderness.

The wilderness holds material wealth as well. There are extensive copper deposits in the interior of French Equatorial Africa. There are heavy reefs of tin, lead and zinc, and exploitation is increasing although mining methods are still primitive. An attempt to develop oil fields fizzled out through shortage of capital; little of the country's ivory is exported and only small amounts find their way to the markets of Europe. There is gold, but its exploitation is left to the old-time prospectors, a bunch of "Jungle Jims," a fair proportion of whom would be greeted by a deputation from the police if they ever set foot in their homelands again. A few hardier souls have established themselves in the interior, where, surrounded by wild animals, including numerous gorilla, and plagued night and day by insects, they produce palm oil and some rubber. Until recently the export of okume, a handsome tropical wood, provided roughly half the country's revenue, but nowadays mineral-ore production is beginning to draw ahead as the leading source of income.

Even the movies have passed French Equatorial Africa by: yet the Belgian Congo is attracting Hollywood's biggest movie makers. I can only guess at the reason. The Belgians see the favors of Hollywood as good business and excellent publicity. The Belgian colonial authorities go stolidly and efficiently to work to help make a success of this spate of films with a Congo setting. The French would seize on a film-making venture as yet another

chance to prove to the world that they are artists to the
tips of their fingers. The making of the movies would be
hindered not because of any difference of opinion between the French and the film makers, but because of
temperamental outbursts, quarrels over the film's "ide-
ology" and kindred intellectual obstacles dreamed up by
the French themselves. Never forget, dear reader, that
to a city-bred Frenchman, whether in Paris, Marseilles or
in African exile, you are a person of inferior intellect,
have no delicacy of feeling and cannot possibly be expected to understand why existentialists should grow
scrawny beards and sit up all night. I have been thor-
oughly indoctrinated in the thought processes of Jean-
Marie and his kind and addresses always beginning in the
same way: "I don't know whether you'll understand
this, but . . ." still break into my dreams.

Another possible reason why Hollywood goes to the
Belgian Congo is that the movement of a large film-
making party in the hinterland of French Equatorial
Africa would be hindered by the almost complete absence of roads, sanitary facilities and the like. Traveling
in the backwoods of the Belgian Congo, though not up
to Pullman standards, is like riding in the lap of luxury
compared with safari conditions in French Equatorial
Africa.

So the country sleeps on, and up in the bush French
settlers with their native "wives" and mulatto children
live out proud, poverty-stricken existences, dreaming of
the soft French countryside, of the Seine and the Loire
they will never see again.

My grandfather could remember the time when the franc was a gold coin. Today 350 francs will barely purchase a dollar. The decline of France as a financial power is part of the unhappy heritage of her colonies. No Belgian from Leopoldville on his way to an outing over at Brazzaville would dream of going to the bank to get his Belgian francs changed. He goes instead to the Leopoldville docks where a herd of Moslems from Nigeria and Senegal, vulture-faced black-market money-changers, operates openly in front of the customs house, offering French francs at discounts up to forty per cent. French money is being discounted in this way in every country I have visited in recent years. French francs will not buy dollars at all, and, dollarless, France is unable to develop her colonies even should she wish to do so.

There is, however, a general lack of enthusiasm for any such projects on the part of the French public, since at the end of the war in 1945 France lay torn asunder, mentally confused, bordering on bankruptcy and in a state of political chaos which since has become a permanent feature of the French scene. The misfortunes of France in three wars since 1870 have contributed in a large degree to the mood of cynicism and desperation which is so evident today from Paris to Saïgon and Martinique. "What is the good of trying to do anything? There will only be another war soon, and that will put us back where we were before." Humbled and bitter, the French people and their ever-changing governments seem to look askance at any ambitious schemes for colonial development.

This attitude is providing the Communists with a great opportunity. The French Communist party is recognized as a constitutional political organization. Not to recognize it would be folly as well as blindness, since, after the Socialists, the Communists are the largest single party in the French Chamber of Deputies, which is the equivalent of the American House of Representatives. With ninety-four out of a total of 627 seats, this powerful unswerving party-line body wields great influence in the French colonies. Communism has much hidden strength in Tunisia and Morocco where it is using nationalist agitation as a means of furthering its own political ends. And it is doing the same in Central Africa.

The economic backwardness of French Equatorial Africa naturally has had an adverse effect on the living standards of the natives. In Brazzaville communism is breeding fast and nothing is being done about it because of that tolerance of communism which is inherent in the French political system. Furthermore, what can one expect when French-speaking native servants and waiters, hanging around to look after the bottle supply while interminable ideological arguments are going on among whites, hear a great deal of comment on communism—not all of it unfavorable—from their self-styled intellectual superiors. This is potentially rich territory, its resources virtually untapped, in fact many of them unsuspected and unknown. Its loss to the free world could be a serious blow, and we have the tragic events in Indochina to hold up as a dreadful example of what can happen when a goodly apple is rotten at the core.

15

Conclusion

THIS BOOK was conceived the day before the worst equatorial electric storm I ever experienced. The brooding heat, the paling sun, the storm-tossed moon, the uneasy stirrings after a sticky, poisonous calm, and the tempest which followed, symbolize Africa's agony today.

One Friday morning in late 1952 I awoke as the last of the mosquito task forces was heading for home. I was covered with bites, and to this day I do not know what kept me asleep, for one mosquito in the room would normally keep me awake half the night. Three weeks before, my landlord had promised me some new mosquito screens, but in Central Africa native notions of time seem to have corrupted even the most industrious of the whites, among whom my landlord could never have been numbered. So I scratched my bites and sulked and finally, in a huff, slammed on my panama and set out to find Oliveira.

Oliveira, known to all as Ollie, was my landlord's

fetch-and-carry boy. His father was a Portuguese trader, his mother a mulatto with a Dutch father—there are many Ollies in those parts. Ollie was supposed to be responsible for the maintenance of the landlord's buildings and their contents, though his inventories were always hopelessly jumbled. He measured the beds and windows for mosquito nets and screens, and if the drains smelled, which they frequently did, Ollie would send along a native boy with a tin of creosote and a piece of rag on the end of a bamboo rod. This load of responsibility sat lightly on him, and he was a born promiser.

The weather was unusually hot. It had been torturingly hot for three days. Damp and heavy, too, as only the equatorial rain forest can be. My thirst didn't improve my mood. I found Ollie in his "office," a bamboo and *matiti* shed set in a clump of anemic-looking banana palms. The roof of the hut was made of shimmering Coca-Cola signs whose possible wanderings had always intrigued me. Inside, slumped in a wicker chair in an atmosphere of creosote, stale vino and black tobacco, sat Ollie. The temperature in the "office" must have been at least 120 degrees.

Ollie was a giant of a man with a neckless head, a wrestler's torso and sparrow legs. A big, top-heavy lout. His face was like the yellow tropical moon, craters and all. The shirt he wore that day was made for the Ituri Pygmy trade: somehow he managed to get it fastened, but he was showing three little ovals of chest and abdomen between the straining buttons. I found myself wondering if he had three little patches of sunburn down his vast front. Of course, he couldn't have had, for Ollie rarely went out in the sun. He hadn't shaved since just before Mass the previous Sunday.

I was prepared for brave promises, an offer of cheap Portuguese wine and some of Ollie's most highly polished flattery. But things did not work out that way at all.

"Ollie," I stormed, "three weeks ago your boss told me he would fix me some new mosquito screens. He said I could have 'em right away. What have you been doing, for God's sake?" I swallowed. "Look, Ollie, if those screens are not in place by tomorrow morning——"

Ollie surprised me by doing something I had never seen him do before: he lost his temper.

"What you think der boss is?" he bawled back at me. "A miracle maker? You think he's made of money to get you all this thing ever time you ask? You think you always get something for nothing?"

A pause. Ollie's rhetoric had exhausted him. The pause lengthened. His anger was evaporating. "Mister," he pleaded. "I gotta lots on my mind. I fix you screens but you gotta wait."

Ollie subsided and reached for his wining jug. I bent forward and knocked it off the table; then I walked out, slamming the door behind me and hoping as I did it that he'd sit and fry. I looked over my shoulder at the mute door and the Coca-Cola signs dancing in the heat. Yes, he might fry at that, I thought. Then I felt foolish. I must watch this heat, I said to myself. It's doing things to my temper again.

Across a vacant lot strewn with worn-out tires and the

carcasses of prewar automobiles lay Armand's bar and poolroom. About this time of day the postmaster generally came out on the post-office steps and shouted for a jug of beer which a native boy carried over on a tray. At about the same time old Martineau would come out of his shipping office to pull down the sun blind. He rarely, if ever, went inside again without calling by for an iced vermouth. But today the world was dead: the native newsboy, sitting on his afternoon papers, was asleep with his neck twisted awkwardly and his mouth open. The off-duty waiter had not bothered to go home, though he was not due to begin work again until six o'clock. He dozed uncomfortably under an awning. An urchin dog came along and sniffed him over but he did not move.

Armand was dozing in his corner by the cash register. The bar counter was deserted: it was too hot and sultry to stand up, and at Armand's we didn't go in for stools. The pool tables lay idle. A customer on his way to the back door had languidly cast three darts at the dart board. One had fallen out and lay on the tiles; the other two hung limply downward. The air was like lead and the big, floppy ceiling fan was protesting as it cut its way through the gray smoke haze. A few flies clung miserably to the wall, moving slowly from time to time to avoid being engulfed in the trickles of moisture. A radio droned lazily in the back room. Dog days of Africa, humid, energy-sapping, fiendishly hot.

At each table in the barroom sat a man. Any other day these men would have been grouped around four, or perhaps five, of the tables; they were regular customers, they were old colonials, friends who had known each other for years. Today each man kept to himself, sullen, awkward and depressed. I went to the bar and ordered a beer.

"It's warm," I said.

Casimir, the Negro bartender, pushed my drink at me and said nothing; he just kept on mopping lazily with his swab. Force of habit—the counter was dry and he worked automatically.

"Give me another," I said to Casimir.

"Sure," he said. Then he added, "Monsieur Adrian tells me it was one hundred and twelve at three o'clock." Casimir retired behind the big ice chest and began to hum *Etoile de Neige* while I looked around.

Fat Carlo Gomez was the only person to take any notice of my entrance. He aroused from his doze, went over to one of the pool tables, removed the cloth and started to knock the balls around in the hope that I would come over and enable him to win some money. But I'd known him for a long time. He surmised I could see through him, so he put his cue back in the rack, hoisted his pants— the crotch seemed to be permanently halfway down his thighs—transferred his free hand to his strawberry nose and scratched it violently as he ambled like a foolish bear back to his seat. Then he leered at me and passed into a coma. The others just sat on. I slid my schooner along the copper counter toward Casimir, pushed through the doors and stood for a moment looking up and down the deserted street.

Outside it was hotter than ever, or so it seemed. The sky had turned gray-blue and the sun was like a lemon behind the haze. The palm trees wilted, the sidewalks were heavy with the turpentine odor of perspiring mango trees. A few weary natives were pretending to work on a half-finished building and the mason's chisel sounded as if it were shaping lead. A dull thud, no echo.

The heat of the sidewalk rose through my shoes; I could feel my feet beginning to swell. Though I made it a rule not to drink before sundown, I found myself hesitating at the entrance to a bar. It was a cocktail bar of sorts which some hopeful landlord, long since dead, had baptised the "Merchant Adventurers." A cut above most bars in the city, the Merchant Adventurers had lively touches of chromium on the stools; there were neat wicker chairs and the walls were not plastered with advertising matter. The Venetian blinds were lowered, there were soft lights and the temperature conditioner was doing a fair job in the circumstances.

I ignored the "hostess," exchanged a grin with the bartender; that was the limit of the exchanges until Fernandes, the copal merchant, came in. Then came Morgado and a bearded American I knew only as "Jungle Jim." We didn't play cards, for we would only have begun to bicker: besides, we had Jim with us and he always won. They say Jim stays in the Congo and over on the French side because he's wanted somewhere in California or Nevada for selling a salted mine to a Jewish syndicate. Somebody started an argument about politics and it was not more than two minutes before fighting words were being bandied around. There was unrest in the air and we were uncertain as to how to handle ourselves. We all felt it: conversation fell to whispers and died, and when we could sit and look at each other no longer we went our separate ways home. It was hotter than ever, for in the Congo the night brings no respite from the heat of the day. The heady wines I had been drinking should have helped me sleep, but no sleep came. I tossed around, keyed up; beneath my skin a tenseness was making itself unbearable.

At about two o'clock in the morning the first whisper came. It was just a faint puff and a shifting of the curtain—a nothing which is everything to those who know. A wave of relaxation washed over me: I knew the storm was on its way. I got up and went outside. The moon high above was still bright but the stars on the horizon shimmered in a slaty haze, which even as I looked at it seemed to rise slowly all around me. It was as if I were trapped in a giant caldron and the smoke from a lazy fire were curling slowly around the rim. Or as if I were in the center of an immense black tulip which was closing up on me, the frayed edges of its petals writhing slowly as it folded.

The lazy rumble of the distant thunder was getting nearer; the first flash of amethyst struck at the tops of the mango trees. The breeze, dead these last days, moved, freshened and within a minute was a gale. The palms bowed low as the wind shrieked through their fronds.

A mango fell at my feet. I picked it up and flung it at a papaw tree, disturbing a fruit bat which whooshed away for shelter. Inside a door slammed, a row of books fell off the shelf; out in the street an outlaw pi-dog howled, there was confusion in Papa Delahaut's chicken roost. The palms bent farther and farther until their trunks became semicircles. Papaw trees were torn up by the roots and hurled into the roadway, mangoes were falling all around me. The song of the cicadas, the eternal symphony of the tropical night, was drowned by the tempest and the creaking of suffering trees.

As the passion of the wind reached its height, the first flurries of rain began to beat down, and while sheets of water began to blot out the background, the wind dropped and the thunder, lightning and rain took over. Forks of lightning kept the sky alive, the silhouetted tails of monstrous clouds seemed to caress the treetops. One peal of thunder ran into another; yet loud as it rumbled and crashed, the edge of the sound was dulled by the deafening hiss of the water. I stood there until I was soaked. It must have been half an hour before I could tear myself away. Then I went inside, dried myself, lay on my bed with a towel around my waist and listened. For a whole hour I lay and listened to the downpour. Sheets of water hammered down on the parched dusty soil: it was as though a dam had burst in the sky and swamped the earth.

Then came the slackening, the end of the tumult and the drip, drip, drip as the sodden trees shed their loads.

The tension had been released in a devastating flood. I had experienced an African storm.

The colonial powers are now living through that tense Friday afternoon, fidgeting, maneuvering and seeking to find comfort where there is little or no comfort to be found. The rest of the world, preoccupied as it has been with myriad troubles and annoyances, may not have felt the premonitory restlessness that has tightened the nerves of the colonial powers. But when the long Friday is over and the storm breaks the rain will drench us all, not merely the colonial powers. Storms are notoriously undiscriminating. And this storm we all began building back in the last century. Its destructive force has had ample time to grow.

The problems of Africa have been bequeathed to the European nations of today by moribund nineteenth-century imperialism. In this study I have tried to indicate that these headaches are no longer the sole concern of the colonial powers: America and the other nations of the free world cannot afford to ignore them if the fight against communism and other "isms" is to be won.

The Belgian Congo, for example, is the world's largest source of uranium, commercial diamonds and cobalt. In his guarded statement in March 1953 Mr. Gordon Dean, at that time president of the United States Atomic Energy Commission, made it clear that the loss to the free world of the Belgian Congo's uranium would be a serious matter. The ores of the Congo are very rich, and although the United States might be able to keep operating on domestic supplies, her inferior-quality ores are much more costly to process. Mr. Dean added that he would not like to say whether or not the expanded plant could be kept fully going. The whole continent of Africa from the equatorial belt southward is rich in precious mineral ores. Northern Rhodesia lies astride one of the greatest copper belts in the world. It was to Central Africa that the Allies had to turn for tin and rubber when the Japanese overran Southeast Asia during World War II.

In Central Africa the Belgians are pursuing an inflexible policy of economic development: benevolent paternalism has rocked the Congolese in a plush-lined cradle which might come apart at the joints under pressure from a developing native political consciousness. The British have tried to find a solution to the African problem in every way. Nigeria and the Gold Coast are on the threshold of self-determination and are separated from backward Kenya, Uganda and Tanganyika by a constitutional gulf. The federation of Northern Rhodesia, Southern Rhodesia and Nyasaland may yet cause untold misery and strife.

The United party of Sir Godfrey Huggins, the Southern Rhodesian Prime Minister, was returned to power by a substantial majority in recent elections, and though Sir Godfrey is a strong federationist—he is in fact one of the formulators of the project—it should not be inferred that his victory is a strong endorsement for Central African Federation on the part of all the people. A disturbing feature of the election is the apparent growth of an opposition comprising some 70,000 immigrant Malanist

Boers, by now mostly well-established miners and farmers, and the right-wing British extremists who believe in "keeping the Negro in his place." It must also be remembered that the native electorate of about 500 has no political influence, fears the opposition and mistrusts the gradualist, very gradualist, black-white partnership policy of the United party. The 6,500,000 voteless Africans are left where they were before—underprivileged "partners" in a scheme which has removed the direct, oftentimes benevolent, influence of the Colonial Office in London and has transferred native affairs to a federal authority dominated by whites. And though Huggins has threatened the Boers and the British extremists with heavy penalties should they foment trouble and has promised a firm immigration policy, the African is, and will continue to be, unsatisfied and chagrined at the trend of events.

Meanwhile the arrogance of the South African Nationalists increases daily. It is primed not only by the writhings of the now almost completely acquiescent United party opposition, but by a wave of increased material prosperity. The extraction of uranium in the Rand gold-mining area is increasing apace; and although not yet in a position to overhaul the Belgian Congo, this mining will nevertheless account for earnings of $100,-000,000 this year and will top $600,000,000 a year ten years from now, according to Doctor Malan. This figure could even be increased should the uranium deposits in the new Orange Free State gold fields prove to be of good quality. The first uranium extraction plant in the Union

of South Africa was opened in October 1952 at Krugers-
dorp in the West Rand. For this event the British and
United States governments are largely to be thanked.
The British government has voted $10,000,000 toward
the project and considerable private capital was sub-
scribed in the United States. Official American blessing
was conferred on the South African uranium-develop-
ment scheme during a visit to the Belgian Congo and
South Africa by the United States Joint Congressional
Atomic Energy Committee in August 1953. In acknowl-
edgment of Anglo-U.S. investments South Africa has
agreed to ship all her uranium to Britain and America, at
least until she constructs her own atomic energy plant.

Anglo-U.S. purchases of South African uranium are
to a large extent conditioned by the necessity of keeping
in the armaments race. As a result South Africa seems to
be on the verge of an unprecedented economic boom,
and a sound national budget will strengthen the hand of
any government. The Malanists, secure in the knowledge
that they are vendors of an indispensable product, continue to wave the stick at the British and have turned
down a United party suggestion that they should pledge
South Africa's continued Commonwealth membership.
Instead they promised friendship to Britain and other
Commonwealth members on their own terms: these were
that Britain and India in particular should cease all criticism of Nationalist racial policies and *should give an
undertaking that Commonwealth membership will not
be extended to any nonwhite autonomous former colonies.* At this rate it seems that South Africa may not

long remain within the Commonwealth, and in this respect it should give further concern to note that Sir Roy Welensky, a tough politician and the leading Northern Rhodesian proponent of Central African Federation, is giving support to Doctor Malan's stand.

Another move which may indicate that the Malanists are completing their plans to strike out on their own was a decision, announced by the South African Minister of Finance recently, to end import control discrimination. Though the removal of strict controls on all dollar imports does not necessarily mean that British and other sterling exporters will be hard hit and though freer international trading may be an end to be desired, South Africa's action may also be seen in the light of an expression of a completely independent financial policy which runs counter to the present inconvertible position of sterling.

Those in Great Britain and elsewhere who hope that by appeasing the South African Nationalists they will be able to hold South Africa within the Commonwealth surely ought to be able to see by now that Malan is completely contemptuous of outside opinion, no matter from whence it may come. He is utterly *immovable* and will not go back, or even appear to go back, on one point of his racial-segregation theory. Even passive resistance inside South Africa will not cause the Malanists to pause and reflect. And, having seen the United party opposition virtually swallowed by the Boer behemoth, leading native thinkers are fearing that the Liberals may meet the same fate. This is unlikely, for the United party was not in any sense a liberal party and did not have to make too great a shift in position to be able to "compromise" with Doctor Malan. There can be no compromise between true Liberals and the Nationalists, and though in their hearts the majority of Africans know this to be true, their leaders, especially those among them who have been politically indoctrinated at the native University at Fort Hare, are becoming rabidly antiwhite. Many of them will not co-operate even with white-dominated Liberal organizations or even with the Communist party which tries desperately to sell them a bill of goods.

The South African situation seems so desperate to me that I hardly raised an eyebrow when a short time ago I read an impassioned plea from a South African Liberal who stated that he was not alone in desiring United Nations military intervention in South Africa. The trouble with police action of this type would be that in the subsequent explosion—which would undoubtedly spread to other parts of Africa—the Communists would make a determined bid for control of the situation and would thus be instrumental in prolonging Africa's agony.

Portugal, the ancient mariner, has remained becalmed while all the other colonizing powers have gone busily about their work. The Portuguese navigators of the late fifteenth and early sixteenth centuries, encouraged in the first instance by their navigator King Henry, put the details of Africa's coast line on the early maps. These early explorers were indifferent colonizers, however, and though Portugal's African Empire has not yet begun to show any sign of approaching disintegration, there is a danger in the present stagnation. Should an investigation of Portugal's colonial development, both economic and social, ever be made by an international body, there is little doubt that something would have to be said about the noticeable lack of management.

The first white man to see the Congo was a Portuguese sailor named Diego Cam, Diego the Bald, who reached the mouth of the river which he called the Zaire in 1482, ten years before Columbus landed in the West Indies. Although an inscribed stone records Diego's visit, the records of the time reveal nothing more. The neglect of Africa was in no small measure due to the discovery and colonization of America, and it was not until after the Revolutionary War that any serious attempt to explore Central Africa was made. The Portuguese, who had devoted much of their time to establishing a vast empire in Brazil, had nevertheless maintained a closer contact with Africa than had the other colonizing powers, and when the era of exploration began in the Dark Continent the Portuguese were already well settled in the territories of Angola and Mozambique.

Graça, a Portuguese soldier of fortune, penetrated into the Congo basin around 1840 and reached the upper waters of the Kasai River, but no claim to sovereignty was made. This Portuguese lethargy continued while the Belgians were boring into the interior from the west. Belgian boats were sailing into the mouth of the Congo along the Angola shore of the river, but little if any protest was made and no competition was offered. Leopold II of the Belgians, encouraged by the United States,

founded his Congo Free State and still no Portuguese reaction was forthcoming. It was not until about 1886,
when Belgium's possession was a fact which the other
European powers found themselves called upon to recognize, that any protest was made against Leopold's achievement. At that time Portugal had held a favored position
on the west African coast for 300 years. When her
clamor, backed by Britain, proved of no avail, Portugal,
torn by political unrest at home, withdrew completely
from the colonial race.

The Portuguese colonies have survived two world
wars. It is a great pity that the Portuguese do not have
the imagination and energy of the Belgians, for their
colonies are fertile and rich in minerals. Mozambique on
the east and Angola on the west have long seaboards and
good harbors at Lorenco Marques, Beira, Loanda, Lobito
and elsewhere which could facilitate the rapid development of the hinterlands of the Portuguese Empire. But
the fortunes, and there are many, which are made in the
Portuguese colonies find their way more or less intact
back to Lisbon. There is not nearly so much plowing
back of wealth as there could be or should be: the individual colonist takes the profits and the Portuguese authorities, though showing every evidence of good will,
are unaccountably slow to buckle to and transform their
African backwoods into progressive, rich and contented
countries. I fail to see why the Portuguese government,
which, although highly authoritarian, has transformed
chaos into prosperity at home under Doctor Salazar, does
not do the same in Africa. The Portuguese citizen is a

good businessman and a shrewd gambler. It defeats me why such things as colonial lotteries are not stepped up (the Belgian colonial lottery is a national achievement) and why development loans could not be floated successfully. The spirit of unrest has not yet been ignited in the Portuguese Empire, but when it is—and it will be— the agitators will make their play on the theme that the "fascist exploiters" are doing nothing to help the native peoples.

It is dangerous to try to suggest a cure for Africa's woes in a few words, but this much can surely be said. The cure is to be found in bringing Africa's native leaders to realize that their evolution to democratic self-government will be a slow and painstaking process. But first these leaders have to be immunized from Communist and other subversive influences by being given a higher standard of living and a sound schooling in moral and ethical values.

Almost all Africans have now seen, and many can employ, the modern devices which make the life of the white so seemingly desirable. The African cannot understand why this pleasant "mechanized" existence should be denied to him. It is difficult to make him realize that he should be educated to the point where he can run his own country on an economically and socially sound basis before refrigerators and washing machines can become a matter of course. The problem is intensified by the time factor, and never was there greater need for intensive action.

And though the old conceptions of empire may be

outworn, it will not help in this period of transition to interpret the granting of more and more power to responsible Africans and Asians as a sign of weakness and disintegration in the colonial powers. There exists a tendency to do just this, and influential sections of the American press are not altogether blameless. Such implications are just what the enemies of the free world can use. Literal-minded Africans easily can be brought by agitators to interpret printed criticism of this type as an invitation to throw out the British, French, Belgians and Portuguese. If a concerted attempt to do this should be made ". . . the peoples of Africa will have cause seriously to consider a joint continental solution," as Manilal Gandhi said; the Communists would step in during the subsequent uproar, and they would make sure that they were in to stay.

I am not an optimist in regard to the future of Africa, or that of any other of the underdeveloped areas, unless the nations of the free world intensify their efforts to set these countries on the road to prosperity and self-esteem. If events in Central Africa continue their present trend, I see a future filled with ever-increasing racial antagonisms and the shedding of much blood.

The old Africa is dying fast; its kings and chieftains are entering history's eternal sleep. In the forests, the farms and the mines a new Africa is being born and the Europeans stand around uncertainly while a many-headed problem infant blinks at the light.

INDEX

INDEX

Labor shortage, Congo, 66
Lakes, Albert, 115, 123, 127;
  Baringo, 229, 230; Edward,
  123; George, 216; Kivu,
  122, 123, 124, 141, 207;
  Nyasa, 152; Victoria, 216;
  Tanganyika, 102, 138, 141,
  207
Labor party, British, 196ff,
  235
Lambaréné, 243
Language statistics, S. Africa,
  180
Laplume, Commandant, 128
Lead, 216
League of Nations, 143
Legum, Colin, 220
Leopard Men, 119
Leopold II, 48, 49, 50, 51, 56,
  69, 70, 125, 128, 136, 262f
Leopoldville, 13, 31, 33, 46,
  47, 57, 65, 66, 67, 69-86,
  89, 91, 93, 96, 98, 102, 107,
  116, 132, 139, 242, 246
Lettow-Vorbeck, Paul von,
  207
Levant, 33
Lianas, 89, 117
Liberal party, S. Africa, 183f,
  260, 261
Libreville, 243
Libya, 33
Limpopo River, 187
Lingala, 88, 90, 95

Livingstone, David, 101, 102,
  151
Loanda, 134, 263
Lobengula, 133
Lualaba River, 47, 48, 131
Lubudi, 138
Lubumbashi, 137
Luo tribe, 238
Lusaka, 191, 199
Lyttelton, Harold, 199f, 219f

Madagascar, 151, 206
Maganga, Chief, 201
Makoko, 15ff, 27
Malan, Dr. Daniel, 35, 42,
  154, 170, 173, 174, 176-180,
  183, 185, 190, 257f, 259,
  260, 261
Malan, "Sailor," 180
Malaria, 17, 70
Malikisi, 230
Mambasa, 121
Mandate, Ruanda-Urundi,
  143; Tanganyika, 207;
  Southwest Africa, 182
Manganese, 62
Mangoes, 78, 253, 255
Maniema, 138
Manono, 138
Mashona, 160
Masuka, 136
Matabele, 160
Matadi, 48, 65, 76, 78; Ma-
  tadi-Leopoldville railway,
  93